The Ineffable Name
A Crafters Guide to Traditional Witchcraft

© George Hares all rights reserved. 2022
© Blair Duncan chapter artwork all rights reserved. 2022
First Edition

ISBN 979-8-8478196-1-9

The following material herein may not be used or reproduced by any means or manner, unless permission is granted by the author George Hares the copyright holder. All permission must be requested and asked to be reproduced by the copyright holders. The same principle applies to the artwork of this book.

The Ineffable Name
A Crafters Guide to Traditional Witchcraft

By George Hares
Illustrations and Artwork by artist Blair Duncan
Photographs Provided by George Bowling
Amazon KDP Self Published
All Hallows 2022

Acknowledgments

I'd like to take this moment to acknowledge and thank a myriad of beautiful entities and people who have contributed to the journey of this book. First of all, I want to Thank the omnipotent, bountiful, jovial king Jupiter as promised for his influence on this body of work. An incredible deal of thanks goes to The White Goddess; Divine Huntress of the Moon and The Black Goddess; Empress and Queen of the Night. Thank you for both being in my life and giving me the ability to step in my own power and trust myself more. I want to thank my best friend, partner, and the talented artist of this book Blair Duncan for his incredible artwork and illustrations which have made the book what it is. It feels such an honour to have your God-given skill inputted into this body of work. It feels like together we've created something beautiful. I would love to thank a really good friend of mine Michelle Harrison who has been completely integral to the journey and development of this book, thank you for all your incredible advice and help. Words cannot sum up just how thankful I am, this book wouldn't be what it is without you. I'd like to take the time to give my thanks to Gemma Gary for her kind words and her input into this corpus of work. Words cannot express my gratitude for your influence. Alongside this, Id like to thank Shani Oates for her advice also concerning this book. Many thanks to my beautiful cousin Susan Hare for being an endless support to me and alongside thanks to my 'Anywhere Coven' who have played a part in my journey (you know who you all are!) Thanks to my sister Eleanor Rose for literally inspiring me with the idea for the front cover design and just being you, you're an amazing person. Thank you, your inspiration has helped forge this corpus of work. In no particular order, I'd like to thank my Craft Brothers and Sisters for their amazing influence on my life and practices. Elena Ramiro Pap thank you for inspiring me to become more empowered within myself and always speak my mind more, truly owning the word witch. You're an incredible friend, and I'm so lucky to have you in my life. Suzanne Swanston thank you so much for the incredible rituals and moments we had together. Ange Simmons for your incredible kindness and beauty, Seth David Rodriguez for your insight as always into the beautiful traditions of Wicca, and for teaching me that Wicca and Traditional Witchcraft are brother and sister.

I'd like to Dedicate this book to the spirits of that very special place. Those spirits and that place enriched every fibre of my being and nourished my soul for years. To those spirits that made my heartbeat faster in fear and excitement, those spirits that enveloped me in their warmth and love. Who made my practice what it is today. May the land be always blessed, always safe, and always protected. And last but not least, to Jonathan Pheonix-Archer with whom I shared those profoundly beautiful experiences with. I'm more than thankful Fate brought us together not only as craft partners, but as friends. The whole time writing this book and being guided by the spirits, I've been reminded of just how special, potent, and sacred those moments truly were. They will stay with me forever.

   George Hares
   -All Hallows Eve 2022

"If you go down into the woods tonight you will be in for a big surprise. Naked, alone, high up in a tree deep in the heart of a wood at dark of night is quite something. For a start, you have left mankind and its brash world behind. Now you are a stranger in the world of nature, the green growing world, where fear is the trigger that releases the spirit force. Like a snail without its shell, you are at the mercy of the smallest gnat – and then it happens. The spirit cloak of darkness descends and enfolds one and you can feel the warmth and protection of the other world. Then it is that you have become aware that there are indeed other places and other things. Some people describe it as the finger of God upon them. Peace, perfect peace. The spirit eyes keep watch over you and you are utterly safe."

                                        – Cecil Williamson

Contents

Foreword By Gemma Gary   11

Introduction   15

So, What Is Traditional Witchcraft?   16
Bodies of Influence: Luciferian, Christian and Pagan   23
Seeking Old Witchcraft   31

Instruments of Arte: The Tools, Their Uses, the Axis Mundi, and The Sabbats

The Tools   39
The World Tree Ritual   46
When Tools No longer Serve You   59
Meditation as a Means for Witchcraft   63
Plants, Herbs and Wortcunning   66
Wortcunning Charm of Farey Hare   69
The Wheel   69

The Witch Gods: Tutelary Deities Worked with on the Cunning Path   77

Yahweh 'Jehovah' The Abrahamic Monotheistic God   78
Tubal Cain and Azazel   79
Rousing the Inner Fire   84
The Queen of Elphame   87
The Devil   91
Old Fate   97

The Liminal World: Spirit Work within the Ways of the Witch   101

Listen to the Land   107
The Mighty Dead and Tapping the Bone   109
The Familiar Spirit   116
Gaining a Faery Counterpart   123
Aquiring an Alraun   126

The Cult of the Witch: Rites and Ritual in the Old Faith   133

The compass round   134
Personal compass Round Rite   137
Elphame's Compass Round   140
Working with the Airts or Winds   141
The Lesser Compass   143
Treading the Mill   144
How to Tread The Mill   146
The Houzle or Bewitched Feast   147
The Houzle Rite   149

Into the Night: Hedge Witchery and Fetch Flight   153

Preliminary Preparations   156
Tips for Achieving Hedge-Crossing   158
Entheogens   165
Chants to Facilitate Fetch Flight   167

Spells and Sorcery: Folk Magic within the Witch Cult   171

Casting Successful Spells   172
Triangle Of Arte   176
The Nine Herbs Charm   179

Dark Moon Bread Poppet 182
To Prepare a Love Potion 183
Cecil Williamson Go Away Doll 184
To Stop Your Man from Being Attracted by Another 184
Image Killing Known as 'Burn the Witch' 185
The Witches Eucharist 185

Conclusion 189

Recommended Reading and Bibliography 199

Foreword by Gemma Gary

Anticipating the arrival of October's end, as the trees redden and the old chimneys of the village awaken with ghostly wood-smoke fingers unfurling forth into the noticeably crisper air, I am busy planning a ritual gathering for Allantide – our rite of the Hallows – the opening of Winter's gates. This particular rite is not the usual 'closed' Allantide rite of our small clan, but an open gathering for those interested in experiencing traditional Craft ritual within a group of the like-minded. As I settle down to write a foreword for *The Ineffable Name* I am prompted to wonder – as the participants of this rite assemble with me beneath old and tangled branches amidst the fields of the Cornish North Coast, what is it that they are looking for? What is it they expect from a glimpse into traditional Craft ritual? What sets the traditional Craft apart?

These are not easy questions to answer, for traditional Craft is something of a wide-reaching umbrella term beneath which we find a range of approaches, forms and 'streams'. And so, there are many possible answers, each partaking of the traditional Craft's common nature or quintessence. *The Ineffable Name* is one of those valuable books in which possible answers may be realised and something of that quintessence explored.

Doreen Valiente – who had, herself, danced within both the 'Circle' and the 'Compass' – employed the term 'traditional witchcraft' to describe both the old-time 'white witches' and cunning folk, as well as those initiatory houses, clans and 'families' claiming origins predating, or concurrent with, the first emergence of Gerald Gardner's revised form of initiatory Craft.

Today the traditional Craft has grown immeasurably – its adherents hailing from all walks of life – and thus its forms and expressions have increased too. Traditional Witchcraft may be recreationist in nature – pursued by practitioners, solitary or in groups, who draw inspiration for their Craft from traditional folklore, mythology, seasonal customs and the operative magical traditions of the old-time cunning folk and 'service magicians.' Today, 'folkloric witchcraft' is becoming a popular and apt term for this type of traditional witchcraft which is often regional in nature, drawing from the traditions, customs and lore of the practitioner's locality. Traditional witchcraft encompasses too those houses, clans and lineages for which pre-Gardnerian origins are claimed and are collectively known as the 'Old Craft.' Notable claimed Old Craft traditions include the Derwent Amber Wove, the Clan of Tubal Cain, the Coven of the Scales, the Cultus Sabbati etc. Brethren and initiates of some Old Craft houses have produced outer writings, in the form of articles and published books, which become source materials inspiring and informing the wider traditional Craft.

A sense of ill-feeling has lingered long between the Gardnerian Craft (and, later, the Alexandrian Craft) and the traditional Craft, a fact that came to a rather ugly head in 1964 with the ill-fated 'Witchcraft Research Assotiation' and its attempt to forge Craft unity. Indeed, similar tensions have long existed between the Gardnerian and Alexandrian Crafts, close cousins though they be.

Fortunately, today, such tensions do appear, little by little, to be easing, aided perhaps by the fact that, by now, there are a greater number of initiates and practitioners of shared and mixed initiatory and experiential backgrounds. It is an often-used phrase – 'that which unites us is greater than that which divides us' – which I feel is true. However, as a practitioner who has been immersed in Gardnerian, Alexandrian, traditional and 'Old Craft' streams, I acknowledge that there are indeed sometimes marked differences in nature between these varying approaches, and yet I see no reason for these differences to result in antipathy nor enmity.

Gerald Gardner, after all, is said to have received initiation into the Craft in 1939. The tradition from which he received this initiation would, of course, have been by its very nature *pre-Gardnerian*. It is claimed also that he later received initiation from Manx Old Craft witches. The Gardnerian Craft and its Alexandrian cousin, therefore, share claimed Old Craft origins. What set Wicca apart, and propelled it to great prominence, was Gardner's vision to establish witchcraft as a pagan fertility religion, accessible to all and in hope that it would, one day, take its place alongside the major religions of the world. Through the publicity Gardner sought and the publicity that sought the Sanders, with the captivating imagery, footage, interviews and articles that resulted, many were drawn to study, to seek initiation and to found covens – the fruit of which is the beautiful and powerful Wiccan ceremonies celebrated in candle-lit and incense-clouded Circles throughout much of the world today. Traditional witchcraft, by contrast, either of the solitary or group kind, had been largely a clandestine affair, maintained as a path undertaken by the few.

Whilst the Gardnerian and Alexandrian Craft streams are, traditionally, coven-based paths – raising power via a dualistic, essentialist concept of male and female polarity via (as far as possible) matched male and female working partners, mirroring in invocation the creative interplay of the witches' God and Goddess.

The traditional Craft, instead, may be solitary in nature (which it quite often is) as well as practiced within groups. Whilst houses, clans and groups have their own ceremonies of initiation, which often differ from the tri-grade initiatory structure, there are also numerous solitary rites of witchcraft initiation found within regional tradition and folklore, often relating to specific *loci* or landscape features, that are adopted and undertaken. Power among traditional Crafters is raised in numerous ways. There is a tendency, in many traditional Craft streams, away from polarity and a dependence upon a partner of an opposing nature to work magic. In such streams, the individual is instead seen as a complete creative being, comprised of inner male-female, light-dark, creative-destructive (and so forth) virtue. Power may come from within, from the land – certain landscape features sometimes being visited depending on the nature of the work – or from tutelary spirits or gods which may be male, female, androgynous or non-gendered, anthropomorphic, theri-anthropomorphic, zoomorphic or without interpreted form. Again, these often arise from the tradition and lore of the region. The Fae may be invoked alongside the virtues of the Saints, Psalms may be spoken or inscribed alongside words of power arising from Christian or Hebraic tradition, but possibly originating in far older beliefs.

The traditional Craft employs a rich and varied methodology – the old service magicians and the lodge, covine or clan alike make use of the time-honoured grimoire tradition and the talismanic arts alongside the magic of the spoken charm, the virtuous wort, the natural amulet and the spells of candle, pin, bottle and cord. With rites and tools that differ from practitioner to practitioner, from stream to stream, the traditional Craft has, as its heart, a working relationship with the eldritch and numinous presences and virtues of place and tide, partaking of the old Mystery of 'All is One'.

Within these pages, George Hares offers an intimate and richly faceted glimpse into a practice that is personal yet draws upon many years of well-honed experience with established traditions, methods and artes of the Elder Craft and Cunning Way.

Herein the reader may learn from the author's thoughts, insights and experiences of many things to be encountered upon the hooks and crooks of the Path, including the traditional Crafter's inner and outer world view, the spirit world and Faery artes, the tools and rites of witchery, the old Gods, the witch's familiar, power, working with the Land, operative magic, and venturing forth across the Hedge of Night. All fertile and potent ground upon which the reader may experiment and from which a personal and workable path of traditional witchcraft may be wrought.

Introduction

So let me guess, you've found out about witchcraft as a practice, and after looking into the many different traditions of the craft, you've noticed a branch of the Witch Cult known as 'Traditional Witchcraft', also known as 'folkloric witchcraft'. Perhaps that's a bit presumptuous of me, and maybe you're a practitioner of another tradition wanting to look more into this area of the tradition, or perhaps you just want to have a cheeky gander. New to witchcraft or not, this book is aimed at the complete and utter beginner when it comes to the beliefs and practices of Traditional Witchcraft. However, within it, you will also find pieces of information to help even the most advanced practitioners develop aspects of their craft, as well as some information on the origins of practice alongside general food for thought. This book will go into the actual beliefs of the tradition itself, and it will reveal things that, in all honesty, I would have loved to have known about when I started delving into Traditional Witchcraft especially in terms of some of the origins of the practices.

This book provides information that goes deeper into references and historical folklore on practices, while also assisting beginners in their path and praxis in general. As always, in my books, I aim to provide information (here's hoping) in a relatable and down-to-earth way. One of the things I noticed, and admittedly struggled with when first venturing on this path, was the use of phrases such as *'The truth lies betwixt the horns'* or *'I am here in the meadow's edge where the goat resides'.* As with a large body of these quotes, the terms themselves can appear quite vague, especially to those venturing primarily on a beginner's path and having had no previous experience with spirituality beforehand. But I'll make the promise that, by the end of this book, you'll know what these two quotes mean as well as be equipped with more knowledge of folkloric witchcraft as a whole.

One of the reasons I'm calling this book *The Ineffable Name* is because the word 'ineffable' describes something too great or too big to even put into words. It means 'indescribable' and 'overwhelming' at times. In my life, the Traditional Craft has made a monumental impact, and the overall sense of belonging I get from the crooked path is too large to even put into words or describe. And so, I genuinely hope, whether you are a seeker interested in pursuing the Old Craft, it can do the same for you as it did for me. To further add to this, the 'ineffable name' is also mentioned during certain invocations within ceremonial magic to call or address spirits infernal or celestial in the name of God.

When first looking at Traditional Witchcraft, many people think that there is an absence of Godhead, but this couldn't be further from the truth. In fact, by the end of this book, you'll see that, while not in a way that the rest of society would deem as 'conventional', the idea and connection with divinity very much does exist.

As another aim of this book, I wanted to create something beautiful, something that, despite being a book for beginners, even the most advanced of witches could pick up and become inspired by to explore different avenues within their craft or to connect with Godhead in a way that deepens their connection to divinity or the spirits. The idea of this book being accessible to beginners but also of use to advanced practitioners further emulates the dualistic nature of the folk witch being someone who can work 'two ways'. I hope this book sparks something of illumination in others' lives and creates something beautiful. As an avid practitioner, I have also learned over the years that there is nothing wrong with going back to basics and sometimes that is exactly what is needed in our craft.

What Is Traditional Witchcraft?

Aims of this book and its goals aside, in essence, Traditional Witchcraft or folkloric witchcraft tends to be (depending on the current) quite simplistic. With this in mind, what exactly is Traditional Craft?

Traditional Witchcraft, or 'trad craft' as it is known, is a beautiful path of witchcraft that bases most of its practices on pre-Gardnerian and pre-Alexandrian Wicca, a modern Neo-

Pagan religion of witchcraft that was created in the 1950s by a man named Gerald Gardner. As such, Traditional Witchcraft incorporates elements recorded from the witch trial confessions dating from the early modern period until the reform of the witchcraft act in 1951.

Many of these confessions were supplied by the actual interrogators themselves and were used as evidence in court. One of the most famous of these accounts came from a woman named Isobel Gowdie, who gave perhaps one of the most detailed witch trial confessions we can find today, complete with charms, spells, and magical formulas, which have had a large influence on witchcraft practices today, especially Traditional Witchcraft. Throughout this book, you will see some of Isobel Gowdie's charms used as examples.

Besides using witch trials as historical sources for inspiration, pieces of folk magic particularly inspired by popular magical practitioners known as 'cunning folk' or 'wise women' have greatly influenced modern Traditional Witchcraft praxis. These folk magicians of the past were often consulted for a wide range of ailments, from curing the common wart to consultations on divination for love and relationships. The cunning folk were an avid part of society and played their roles by helping those within the community.

Originally, however, had you mentioned the word 'witchcraft' to a cunning person, they would not have reacted positively at all. If you were called a witch, it did not only ensure that you ended up at the gallows, but it also meant that they believed your soul belonged in hell and that you had sworn allegiance to infernal powers. Conversely, cunning folk worked with the Christian God rather than the Devil and were employed to counteract maleficia. However, the terminology of 'witch' changed dramatically throughout time, and its definition depends on the period, which is another aspect to be mindful of when doing research as well as engaging in conversation and practices regarding the terminology of the word 'witch'.

Another large body that heavily influences Traditional Witchcraft is folklore told by many through the ages. This may be a folk story regarding a certain landscape or place that connects with the Devil, inspiring the practitioner to venture to that place tied to the Old One to work with the Witch Lord himself in ritual. Another method of utilizing lore is by reading tales that tell of ways in which a witch created a spell. Such a tale may inspire a practitioner to utilize such a method as a basis for a conjuration or charm.

With this approach, these practices will differ greatly from one practitioner of the Old Craft to another. They may share similarities, as they will be likely working with older lore and traditions and incorporating ritualistic aspects of Traditional Witchcraft, such as laying a compass round. However, even the actual rite for laying a compass round and various other aspects of ritualistic witchcraft will differ from practitioner to practitioner. This again reiterates the beauty of individuality, as well as the absence of dogma that most Traditional Witches will experience.

Quite often when it comes to magical practices, the Traditional Witch will look at and take inspiration from older sources of folk magic. This might be, for example, an artifact from the Museum of Witchcraft and Magic in Boscastle or older literature such as Reginald Scot's *The Discoverie of Witchcraft*. They may then either perform such a charm or ritual as described in the old lore or even adapt it to suit the needs of the individual.

However, when we look at the older sources we have of witches, be it from magic, history, and lore. It's not uncommon to find many references to influences that some might consider dark or even sinister to a degree. This is part of the reason why some aspects of this path and its praxis incorporate the use of working with bones and skulls, necromancy, left-hand ideology, and even workings with the folkloric Devil. I want to add the disclaimer that the latter is *very* different from the Christian Satan, so put your crucifixes away! We will get more into this in due time.

Lights Black Majesty: Embracing Darkness

Consequently, there are aspects of Traditional Craft that may evoke fear in some: the embracing of and working with the darkness. This is something that is seen and has been demonstrated in a myriad of books. One in particular that springs to mind is Gemma Gary's incredible work *The Devil's Dozen,* which I thoroughly recommend to any witch working with the folkloric Devil. One of the workings mentioned is known as 'All is One'. In this rite, the practitioner ventures into a dark and lonely wood strips off all garments, and lays on the floor, allowing themselves to give into that fear and eventually becoming overtaken by it and accepting the darkness. This is an exercise originally given by Cecil Williamson, the original creator of what we now know as the Museum of Witchcraft and Magic in Boscastle.

In the days of the old, the village would always be a place of order and structure. A society with its rules and regulations and the community would have created for themselves a 'safe space', a place where they were in a sense secure from the wilderness. Just over from the village would be a boundary that separated this created order from the woods, a place with no rules, no structure, a place full of wild animals, where morals didn't exist. The village had no control over this, and so, many feared these woods. However, historically, be it in folk tales, accounts, or lore, the witch was known to reside on this boundary, standing betwixt order and chaos, never fully fitting in but always at the edge of the community.

As such, the witch is a being who actively chooses to embrace the darkness. The witch chooses to become overwhelmed with fear until it is joined by acceptance as well as understanding and gnosis. So much beauty is to be experienced in the dead of night, so much understanding, and so much connection to be made with the otherworld. Within Traditional Craft exists this idea of gnosis, coming from the ancient Greek noun 'knowledge', which means gaining knowledge of spiritual mysteries. To many, gnosis is achieved by various forms of techniques that normally take place during the day. However, to the witch, what better way to achieve gnosis than to shut out the mundane daily hustle and bustle, stop the loud noises of the day, and lie in the stillness of the black night? It is only when darkness encompasses us that we can truly see and experience illumination through the powers of witchcraft. The famous Witch of Kings Cross, Rosaleen Norton wrote a poem about the darkness, and quite honestly, there is something so deeply touching and beautiful about it:

"Light's Black Majesty: Midnight Sun: Lord of the wild and living stars; Soul of magic and master of Death;
Panther of Night… enfold me.
Take me, dark Shining One; mingle my being with you
Prowl in my spirit with deep purring joy,
Live in me, giver of terror and ecstasy,
Touch me with tongues of black fire.
Night, freakish night sets me free."

Despite it appearing 'darker' or at times more 'sinister' than other witchcraft practices, time spent with and immersed in the darkness can have an utterly illuminating effect. Words cannot say just how beautiful, rewarding, and empowering it is to walk upon the crooked path. When they speak of the crooked path, by the Gods, do they mean it! The path you tread is crooked, it has twists and turns and isn't as strait-laced as some might prefer.

The path itself is not for everybody, and that's ok. What works for one doesn't have to work for another. So if Traditional Craft isn't someone's cup of tea, it doesn't mean they're not 'dark enough' or not 'worthy', as has unfortunately been claimed in some other works. Such a statement is elitist and quite frankly absolute cobblers. It just means that path isn't for them, just like its sister branch of witchcraft known as Wicca is not for everybody either I can certainly attest to that. With this in mind, if you are a beginner embarking upon the path of witchcraft, it's important to mention here that Traditional Witchcraft is *not* the only form of witchcraft.

Old Craft vs Wicca

Other witchcraft traditions and sects exist, and one of the most prominent of those is the previously mentioned Wicca. Unfortunately, among some practitioners of the Old Craft tradition, there tends to be an intense dislike towards Wicca as a practice. Strangely enough, this dislike can also be seen historically: Cecil Williamson, for example, had a strong dislike towards Wicca as a practice and frequently criticized it as a tradition. Robert Cochrane, a character whom we will get into more detail throughout the book, also had an incredible aversion toward the tradition.

I have to confess, that I as a practitioner was once guilty of this too back in the day. But one only needs to scratch the surface and read about the history of the practices to see that Wicca has influenced Traditional Witchcraft and vice versa. They have both added richness and vitality to each other, and although many don't know this, have unknowingly worked side by side. Wicca has given Traditional Craft more recognition and created an awareness of modern witchcraft practices in general for the general public. Like it or not, they coexist and their origins are conjoined. I like to see them as sister beliefs: they are related to each other, but they're not the same person and both are individuals in their own right. As such, each is equally as valid as the other path of witchcraft.

One belief that is often central to practitioners of Wicca and other forms of modern witchcraft but is not adopted by the majority of those who practice the Old Craft, is the concept of 'Harm none' and the threefold law.
While the idea of the threefold law within this current of witchcraft is often believed to be a rule integral to Wicca itself, the first mention of the threefold law can be found in the novel *High Magic's Aid* written by Gerald Gardner, which states: *"Thou hast obeyed the law. But mark well, when thou recievest good, so equally art bound to return good threefold."* Further mention of the law of 'harm none' was then published by Raymond Buckland in 1968, and in 1975, put into a poem by Lady Gwen Thompson, known as *'The Rede of the Wiccae'* which later became incorporated into the witches creed by Doreen Valiente. However, aside from this information, the threefold law, and the law of harm none, isn't something that was traditionally found within the religion of Wicca.

When talking in terms of rituals and length of spells done within Traditional Witchcraft, they are usually performed in a much shorter timeframe than what is usual in its sister belief Wicca or other occult practices. From experience, a lot of rituals might take an hour in other traditions or so, but a Traditional Witchcraft ritual or working will normally take around 20 minutes to complete the compass round rite is normally done within minutes if that. That doesn't mean they are more effective or more 'worthy' than occult practices. Some enjoy the lengthy rituals and the psychodrama. When it comes to spirituality and occult practice, different people connect to different things. And once again, what works for one, won't necessarily work for another. By the way, as a heads up, you'll hear that expression *a lot* while reading this book because I want to stress just how important personal practice is.

In comparison to its Wiccan sister, Traditional Witchcraft workings tend to take place outside in nature rather than indoors. That's not to say that Traditional Witchcraft rites *can't* take place indoors, as they do. However, a large amount of the time, Traditional Witchcraft rites are preferably performed outdoors. When concerning covens also known as 'covines' or 'coveens' in trad craft, they are known more often as 'robed covens' to delineate them from their Wiccan cousins who typically practice 'skyclad' or naked.

Karma, threefold Law, and Personal responsibility

The threefold law is connected to the idea of karma, which is most commonly considered an eastern concept and as such does not play any part in Traditional Witchcraft. Instead, practitioners of the Old Craft tend to make use of the concept of personal responsibility. This means, that if you cause a spell or a charm to happen, then you need to be able to take full responsibility for it. In layman's terms, let's look at a situation where this might apply.

Sarah is pretty pissed off at work, her boss is doing her head in. Sarah has a pretty bad temper, so in her rage and at that moment, she creates a doll of her manager and stabs the doll with glass repeatedly into its stomach area. A couple of weeks pass and Sarah's manager is caught in a violent accident and is stabbed repeatedly. Sarah is more than upset, and tries everything in her power to save her manager. She realizes she should have tried something far less severe, but it is too late. Her manager survives but sustains lifelong injuries that can never be undone.

In terms of personal responsibility, Sarah didn't think her actions through. She knows she wouldn't stab her manager, or anybody for that matter repeatedly, and couldn't live with herself after completing such an act. Now, Christ on a bike, this example is a bit of a dramatic scene, and it doesn't mean by stabbing someone's image in the stomach they will automatically become stabbed in "real life", but it's important to carefully consider one's magical actions beforehand. Witchcraft aside, personal responsibility and accountability are generally great things to have, be it one's self, the world, or people in general. Society would hold much more of a balanced judgment, and be more mindful if people stuck with these practices.

Considering practices that seem a bit 'darker' and tying them to the aspect of personal responsibility, it would come as no surprise that within Traditional Craft there is no 'harm none' rule at all. Like it or not, an incredibly large part of the history of witchcraft is cursing, being able to inflict harm and do damage. This is one of the many reasons that witchcraft as a practice has such a nefarious reputation. To the community, Witchcraft in the early modern period was not a good or beneficial practice that revolved around sending positive energies to others. Instead, it was believed to be a practice to blight others' crops, kill cattle, and harm others within the community. That's not to say Traditional Witches seek to create chaos, but historically, at one point, that's what being a witch meant to the community within the early modern period.

Bodies of Influence: Luciferian, Christian and Pagan

One large influence that goes into Traditional Witchcraft and its 'mish mash' of different belief systems is that of Luciferianism and the left-hand path. So, what exactly does that mean? Well, let's look at the explanation of

Luciferianism and what it entails. The name Lucifer means 'light bearer' but is also translated as 'morning star'. This is why Venus, being the morning star, is often connected to Lucifer, and his name as 'day star' can even be found in the texts from Isaiah as seen below. Luciferianism is a belief system that venerates and idolises the characteristics and traits that are affixed to Lucifer. Further note that this system venerates characteristics rather than the actual entity itself. The main goal of Luciferians in general is that of enlightenment through the highlighting of truth, freedom of will, worshipping the inner self and reaching one's personal potential.

The story of Lucifer goes as follows: Lucifer was the most beautiful angel within the angelic hierarchy, and because he became so impressed with his own beauty and intelligence, he didn't want to abide by rules that were imposed onto him through no choice of his own. He was resentful to follow these rules delegated to him by God, and so as an act of his own free will, he defied God. And because of this, he was cast out of heaven. The text from Isaiah quotes:

> *"How you are fallen from heaven, O Day star, son of dawn! How you are cut down to the ground, you who laid the nations low! You said in your heart, 'I will ascend to heaven; above the stars of God I will set my throne on high; I will sit on the mount of assembly in the far reaches of the north; I will ascend above the heights of the clouds; I will make myself like the most high.' But you are brought down to Sheol, to the far reaches of the pit. Those who see you will stare at you and ponder over you: 'Is this the man who made the earth tremble, who shook the kingdoms, who made the world like a desert and overthrew its cities, who did not let his prisoners go home?" (Isaiah 14:12-17)*

Lucifer in this tradition isn't necessarily the Christian Satan but rather a liberator or, going by his true name 'light bringer', he acts as an illuminator. He sheds light even in the darkest corners of the world showing us what is truly 'hidden'. Considering that the term 'occult' means 'hidden', Luciferianism and Traditional Witchcraft really work well together. Lucifer is a rebel, who acts as an adversary to rules and regulations, who does not blindly follow rules that aren't fully beneficial or useful to everybody.

It is not only Lucifers story or mythos that is embodied, but we also see an acknowledgement of other figures that walk on the fringes of God's acceptance, such as Lilith the woman who refused to lay under a man. Instead, she wanted to lay on top and so was banished by God. Cain, the first farmer and murderer, was banished by God because of his crime against Abel. More notable, we see Tubal-Cain who had inherited Cain's sin of murder by being able to create weapons out of forge and flame, which in Gods eyes was seen as a means to facilitate the act of murder.

These figure heads which play their roles within the current of Traditional Witchcraft, all have one thing in common: they never fitted in and, in fact, were overly defiant. "No, I will not obey the rules, I will go by my own. No, I will not let a man lay over me and claim me, I'll claim him." They become figure heads of the way of the witch, not necessarily with their actions, but rather through their defiance and search for personal gnosis. The witch never fitted in and actually mostly went against conformity. The witch was somebody that lived on the very edges of society, living their own life to their own rules rather than by somebody else's delegations.

Older Craft?

So, with all this said, exactly how old is Traditional Craft? Does it predate the practices of Traditional Wicca? To give not exactly clear-cut answers to both these questions: perhaps. And I'll explain why:

You see, witchcraft in general, of course, will predate Wicca. It's an out and out denial to suggest otherwise when we have all this evidence in literature and lore as well as artifacts of folk magic left behind in history. One needs only to go down to the Museum of Witchcraft in Boscastle or read a book to see that witchcraft as a practice has existed long before Wicca. We also see in history, the existence of characters such as George Pickingill of Canewdon, who was an Essex cunning man who allegedly said he had run nine witch covens and would instil fear in the locals and others around him at the time. Another example is that of Cecil Williamson himself, who was also very open about his practice and regularly spoke about the 'Aunt Mays' or wayside witches of the west. The museum also holds artifacts such as dolls struck with pins and poppets hanging from rope, etc. The evidence shows quite clearly that, prior to Wicca, people were practising a form of witchcraft. The spells and charms used within Traditional Witchcraft, such as witch bottles, witches' ladders, doll and pin magic etc, all tie to older forms of folk magic that would have been practised by these 'Aunt Mays' as Cecil came to know them as.

Old Craft Lineages

However, the use of ritual structure in Traditional Witchcraft such as the compass round, treading the mill, the houzle as well as a lot of rituals that may be deemed 'ritualistic witchcraft' rather than 'operative witchcraft' are all things that are for the most part new to witchcraft compared to older practices of folk magic. Yes, they may take from older sources and be influenced by them, but their genuine origins as a whole complete practice cannot be claimed to go back hundreds of years and having been passed down by covens of witches. Please bear in mind, however, that this book hasn't been hand copied from generation to generation with leaves and herbs pressed into it carefully over the years to hold within ancient spells from an old and secret coven. This book is a mix of old and new, much like the tradition of Traditional Witchcraft itself. The newer rituals mentioned above do give 'structure' to the practice of Traditional Craft and do (in my opinion) help it to become more of a living and breathing tradition. These rituals were primarily created by a man known as Robert Cochrane, also known as 'Roy Bowers', who, in the 1960s, was the magister of a Traditional Witchcraft coven which was named the 'Clan of Tubal Cain'.

Robert Cochrane circulated a lot of rumours that he had Old Craft lineage to 1734, which was disputed by another member of the coven, Doreen Valiente, known also as 'the mother of witchcraft' as she did at the time stand between Wicca and Traditional Craft, having spent time in both traditions. According to Valiente, the clan's rituals were a lot more spontaneous, shamanic, and there wasn't as much structure and order to them as there was in Wiccan rituals. Robert Cochrane did have a lot of animosity towards Wicca as a tradition, which is evident within the Robert Cochrane letters. If anybody is interested into looking into this branch of craft, then I strongly suggest to read The Star Crossed Serpent volumes by Shani Oates and Evan John Jones. Furthermore, to this, I also recommend reading the various writings of Robert Cochrane such as the letters and articles, supplied by the Clan of Tubal Cain website.

Additionally, other currents of Traditional Craft came to light and influenced what we now practice in the modern day and age. One example is the Cultus Sabbati, also known as Sabbatic Witchcraft, brought about by Andrew Chumbley. This is form of witchcraft that takes deep influence and inspiration from the witches sabbat, a meeting of witches documented in witch trials. Such a meeting involved a group of witches and imps alike, feasting, fornicating, and engaging in various revelry. A large part of this also was communing with the Devil. Andrew Chumbley describes Sabbatic Craft as such:

> "'Sabbatic craft' describes a corpus of magical practices which self-consciously utilise the imagery and mythos of the 'Witches Sabbath' as a cipher of ritual, teaching, and gnosis. This is not the same as saying one person practises the self-same rituals in the self-same manner as purported early modern 'witches' or historically attested cunning folk, rather it points toward the fact the fact that the very mythos which had been generated about both 'witches' and their 'ritual gatherings' has been appropriated and reorientated by contemporary successors of cunning craft observance and then knowingly applied for their own purposes."

In my opinion, it's important to talk about the historical age of Traditional Witchcraft as the actual term itself can be misleading. To me, as much as I still use the term 'Traditional Witchcraft' or 'Old Craft', I see how the terminologies can seem problematic to some, so I'm more comfortable calling it 'folkloric witchcraft'. I personally think this term allows for a more precise definition. However, for the sake of teaching you the different terms that people use to describe Traditional Witchcraft, such as 'the Old Faith' or 'the Witch Cult,' I have included them herein.

In terms of historical accuracy, most things we're doing within the craft are linked to older sources and older forms of praxis, particularly when it comes to folk magic. This especially refers to older charms, such as the witch bottle. As you will also see in this book, I have included a selection of spells and charms which have been taken from older sources. However, despite having older roots, the ritualistic side of these practices is in fact younger than those of the Wiccan tradition, which is absolutely ok!

It seems sometimes we get carried away by the idea that what we practise must be hundreds of years old but why? Does the age of the tradition itself validate our practice to some unconscious degree? Just because a working we do is old, does not automatically mean it will be successful. The most important thing, when it comes down to our own practice, is that our magic works, and above all, that one becomes connected to the spirits of our craft and Godhead. That's the most important thing in our own personal praxis, not how old or ancient something is or whether it's been passed down from generation to generation.

Again, investigate the origins of things and look at references, but if something isn't as old as you thought it was but you get a genuine connection out of it and it *adds* to your practice, then why the hell not incorporate it? I've seen some people in the past throw the baby out with the bath water, so to speak, and it's upsetting to see. Of course, references are important as it gives credit where credit is due, but do not get so obsessed with references that you end up down an extremist pathway chucking everything out to the point you're left with nothing in your own practice, all the while slating down anybody that doesn't do the same thing as you do. Don't be that person, no one wants to be them.

When it comes to modern witchcraft traditions, we often heavily associate the word 'Pagan' with modern forms of spiritual belief (particularly in the west). Traditional Witchcraft is also, to a degree, Pagan and as such holds Pagan elements within it: the incorporation of the fae folk, practising within stone circles and burial mounds, in desecrated churches (we know that a majority of churches were built upon Pagan places of worship), working with Old Gods the list really could go on here. However, it's remarkably curious that there are some Traditional Witches that do see themselves as Pagan and there are some that don't necessarily see themselves as fully Pagan or even Pagan at all. As mentioned before, there is a blend of other beliefs within Traditional Witchcraft, such as elements of Luciferianism.

Christianity's Influence

We can also find elements of Christianity as working with older forms of folk magic within Traditional Witchcraft takes from the practices of the cunning folk, who most of the time were Christian and so incorporated psalms and saints into their magical operations. However, this doesn't mean all Traditional Witches will feel comfortable with merging Christian elements into their practice. I know plenty of Old Craft witches that will not work with saints or Christian prayers and instead will adapt older charms to suit a more Pagan practice. Two primary entities we will often work with will be the Queen of Elphame and the Devil. What's interesting is that during this time the were mentioned, Christianity was the main dominant religion in the British Isles alongside the rest of Europe. However, the Queen of Elphame was the queen of faeries and played a major role within the structure of witchcraft and a part within witch trials by facilitating the accused witches' otherworldly experiences. The Devil also plays a key part in witchcraft historically. In this sense, we can therefore see a large crossover between Christianity and the older Pagan faith which is evident in older texts and artwork.

An example is an illustration from 1629 named *Robin Goodfellow: His Mad Pranks and Merry Jests* which portrays the Devil as a faery figurehead, holding a taper and broom with an erect phallus whilst a group of people dance around him in a circle. Robin Goodfellow is also termed as Puck, Bucca, or a hobgoblin of some sort, essentially a faery spirit. However, it is easy to see the imagery of this illustration and its connection to the imagery of the witches sabbat. Revelry, dancing, the playing of instruments, circles, and last but not least the goat-like God carrying a broomstick over his shoulders, bearing an erect phallus whilst holding a lit taper candle, in the centre of this activity, overseeing it and acting as the main figurehead for the evening's festivities. If you ask me, this illustration could EASILY be a coven of witches dancing round the Devil during the sabbat. In fact, during this publication there is a mention of somebody who gets Robin Goodfellow mixed up with the Devil:

"The gentlemen cried out for help, for he thought that the Devil had been to fetch him for his wickedness. But his crying was In vaine for Robin did not carry him into a thick hedge."

We once again see a reference here from this publication acknowledging the existence of the Abrahamic God whilst also linking Robin Goodfellow with charitable elements and helping those poorer in the community and in need, much like a God would provide for their people or followers:

"Robin shaped himself like the tapsters brewer, and came and demanded twenty pounds which was due to him from the tapster. The tapster, thinking it was the brewer paid him the money which money robin had gave to the poor of the parish before the tapsters face. The tapster praised his charity very much and said that God would bless him the better for such good deeds. So after they had drunk with one another, they parted."

Whilst these older sources still hold acknowledgment for the Abrahamic God, to my mind there is also a subtle hint of other beings having Godlike attributes to them. We see the Queen of Elphame being the queen of the faery and aiding the witch in her otherworldly actions and experiences, alongside the Devil also playing an integral role to the witches' initiations giving them powers and spirit allies through pacts.

With this in mind, one does wonder whether or not these were the 'other Gods' of the older Pagan faith that have been demoted to some degree from their deity status to that of 'faery folk', or to quote from the accusers of the witch trials, 'wicked spirits'. Perhaps these spirits were just older Gods and were acting as the Gods of the oppressed? The Gods of those who were relegated in society and didn't fit in? I mean those relegated as in those who were seen as threats, who fought against dominion and regulations. Please be aware, the latter statement isn't a fact, but its food for thought, nevertheless.

Seeking Old Witchcraft

With all this being said, were witches even real? Or was it a fabrication told and made up by those higher up to instil fear? Firstly, let's look at some of the attitudes that many had during the time of witches and their role within society. The entity known as the witch, was seen by members of early modern society as a scapegoat for all that went wrong within the community. If livestock had died then a witch had cursed your cattle, if your partner had gotten sick it was due to him angering a witch, if you had suffered misfortune then you were cursed by an evil eye. The beliefs in the invisible world and its influences particularly within the early modern period were extremely prevalent within society. So much so, that various steps such as apotropaic folk magic were taken by regular folk to ensure the protection of the community against the witch and her nefarious antics.

To be called a witch in the early modern period was something to be feared greatly, it would ensure ostracism from the entire neighbourhood around you as well as possibly sending you to the gallows. The accusation of witchcraft would also generate business for some in the community such as cunning folk or those in which we now would term 'white witches' (a term that become popular in the late 1800s to early 1900s). The cunning man would also help a person identify the witch who in some cases, when convicted in court would involve the cunning man's presence to testify in certain instances.

Then there were characters that would exploit fear in the community to earn a quick shilling and act as 'witch finders'. An absolutely revolting character was known as Matthew Hopkins or the supposed 'witch finder general' in Essex and East Anglia who would interrogate other 'witches' putting them to trial, and in return earning an absolute fortune. Nine times out of ten I don't think many witches were caught at all, Matthew Hopkins just put innocent people to death, he was an out and out murderer in my opinion guised under a cloak of righteousness and armed with an army of fanatical crusaders.

I realise I'm entirely about to express an unpopular opinion but hear me out, as I believe there is always some information to this point many miss out. To many academics, there holds an agreed opinion that witches didn't exist and were innocent people that were either scapegoated or that accusers were actively hallucinating due to something known as 'ergot poisoning'. This is caused by a bacteria grown on mouldy bread and cereals which many would have typically been exposed to. In my opinion, there is truth in this and in some cases absolutely I think that absolutely played a part, but what if ergot poisoning played a part in somebodies experience who was avidly having a spiritual journey and flying to the sabbat?

When most academics mention ergot poisoning, they often think of the accusers themselves that are seeing Margaret down the road riding on a broomstick in flight to a mountain in order to visit the Devil, but what if rather than the accusers seeing this, it was actually Margaret HERSELF i.e.: the accused? Its food for thought certainly.

We see in witchcraft this idea of flying ointment which was compounded of various ingredients most in which were incredibly poisonous but also contained hallucinogens. It was a salve in which the practitioner of the black arts was said to rub onto their skin and take flight to the sabbat or to the invisible world to meet with familiar spirits or the Devil. This recipe is found in different texts throughout the early modern period in history. It gives us an outsiders look that with these plants and ingredients being hallucinogens, the flying we saw wasn't as physical as many believed it to be, that it perhaps would have been spiritual. So, if we see the use of entheogens historically as a means to facilitate spirit flight, then what is the difference between mouldy bread that gives the person visions of the otherworld? It may have been accidentally rather than purposely compared to flying ointment, but it is ultimately still ingesting the use of toxic substances that cause severe hallucinations.

Another aspect of this is that so many similarities are seen in terms of confessions when we look into witch trials during the early modern period. The knowledge and similarities of the sabbat, the similarity that ensued in rituals such as renouncing your baptism, the entities met during these experiences such as the Devil and various acts that came along with these interactions. The similarities between different trials are all there, they may differ in detail but ultimately the similarities are overwhelming for it to be a coincidence.

Even if it were a coincidence or just a by-product of the mentality and beliefs towards witches in general, everyone knew that there were certain acts that witches performed and gained supernatural powers to injure, kill, or gain food such as witch Susannah Edwards, who in 1682 came across a familiar who when approaching her asked her whether she was a poor woman upon whose reply the familiar replied that *'she need never want again for meet or drink or clothing.'* This sentence that was quoted to her upon their first meeting, is reminiscent of the times people were in and the harsh environment that people faced.

Desperate Times Call for Desperate Needs

These were incredibly delicate times, where one simple illness could completely throw off your family's security in terms of eating and drinking, in terms of keeping your house. Things like illness without the medical progressions we have today were so predominant within early modern society. With this in mind, in the 1600s the population of England was just roughly over five million people alone that's not including Scotland, Wales or Ireland. Bear in mind we're not even considering populations in the rest of Europe in terms of numbers and figures.

My point here is, if all these people living in such harsh conditions and quite frankly desperate times, knew and had some amount of knowledge on witches and their practices. Hearing how some witches were renouncing their faiths and some of the rites during trials through news or village gossip, whilst believing witches had access to power that helped them then desperate times call for desperate measures. Out of all those people during that time, there would have been at least one person that would have attempted these things in order to facilitate and gain the powers of witchcraft. So you're telling me that with the combination of the desperate and severe times, the population of people, conjoined alongside the common folk knowledge and belief known, that NOBODY practised witchcraft? Stop yourself.

There would have been some people at some point during the early modern period practising some form of witchcraft in some way. It may not be what we have in mind when we think of witchcraft, but I do feel like witchcraft as a practice did occur.

Now don't get me wrong, with this statement please don't rush into thinking I'm going to start quoting Margaret Murray's book God of the witches, or believing that the sabbat actually physically happened and people came from all over and met up in different covens, or that witchcraft was an underground persecuted Pagan cult that survived various reformations.

All these thoughts are within rational reason. I'm not in any way shape or form, implying that I believe that most of the people they caught were practising witches. But, in my opinion, some witches gave confessions such as Isobel Gowdie that to me there is too much knowledge given there of spells and charms etc.

It's so important to be mindful at the same time that people were under torture and that torture in early modern

Scotland compared to England was legal at the time and these of course are contributing factors. As I think we need to evaluate all the information given and be practical rather than just one side. However, I think people were practicing some form of witchcraft in some format. I don't think they were attending secret meetings during the night with a coven. I don't think every village or place had a person who was practising or that witches were a major occurrence everywhere, but I think out of the whole of Europe in that time period more than a handful of people would have been practising something.

Regarding what academics say and quote is incredibly important, and it's extremely valuable information given so I want to make it perfectly clear that I am not disputing what evaluations they are making at all. I just think that given the time period, it seems highly unlikely to me that nobody would have been practising witchcraft at that time and a person practising witchcraft didn't exist at all. To my mind when you think of it in terms of the demographics, the background of the environment people was exposed to, such a suggestion of there being absolutely no witchcraft existing at all in a time where the belief in folk magic was so prevalent, seems almost insane to me.

However, I do want to add onto these arguments, that realistically academics and others like myself weren't in the early modern period so we don't really have a concrete view on what occurred. And I think that's an avid point to be mindful of. However, with all these factors and points of view in mind, I consider it's incredibly important for me to clarify that I want the reader to make up their own minds on this, but it is also crucial for the reader to make your mind up based on facts of what we know rather than based on fiction.

In relevance to historical accuracy, I want to add a disclaimer to this book for those who may still be unaware. Traditional Witchcraft as a practice is not something that has been handed down from generation to generation. If you're expecting this book to be something that's been copied from my great grandmother who comes from a long line of witches you're sadly mistaken. It's a mix of all things here, old and new which adds to its uniqueness, its beauty and a practice connecting with the local land spirits around us, helping us build otherworldly companionships with familiar spirits, elevating our ancestors and tapping into different aspects of Godhead that it changes and impacts our lives, and ultimately assists us making this practice and the experiences that come with Traditional Witchcraft, truly Ineffable.

Instruments of Arte: The Tools, Their Uses, the Axis Mundi and the Sabbats

Within the Old Craft current, tools are often used but for the most part, they can entirely depend and vary on regional praxis with different practitioners and with personal preference to the crafter. I've known of different working groups across the UK that use tools they feel correspond to their areas. A ritual I once attended in Norfolk utilised a pitchfork, a scythe, and some sheers as ritual tools. This emphasised the main agricultural tools within that land, as a way to further connect with the spirits of place.

The tools are effectively used to assist the witch in their workings when connecting to the spirit world or the witch Gods. However, there has been a debate with a myriad of witches over the years. Some question whether or not the tools are just tools or if they themselves also add power to the rituals, and really, for the most part, I think it's down to what you yourself believe.

The tools for me are used as tools to help assist the witch with their arte and craft, however, not all Traditional Witches will use all of these tools mentioned and in fact, may have a completely different set of working tools pertinent to the practitioner. I'm just trying to mention the large majority of the tools one will typically find with a practitioner of the Old Craft. As an animist, I do certainly believe that the tools have their own spirit and of course where they are collected or gathered will carry with them power and virtue from the land stored, which the practitioner can work with effectively in their rites. It is within my opinion that it is important to mention this, and of course, they will have their own spirit and their own energies too that can be worked with.

However, in the same breath (and I'm going to be very frank) I've seen many a practitioner explain: but you HAVE to have this and that…. Well, why? My own personal practice is my own PERSONAL practice and I can incorporate whatever I want within it. If I'm not comfortable with not using a certain tool I don't have to justify that to anybody, when it comes to my own practice what's important is that its what matters to ME and that if the tools I use work effective magic and forged a connection to the invisible world, that's the main thing that matters.

I've seen many practitioners with so many different arrays of tools that are beautiful but they hardly utilise them within their craft. I think sometimes we can have it in our minds that we have to have or own a certain tool in order to cast effective magic but actually in actual fact, it is about finding what works for yourself and what works for you. Sometimes owning too many tools can actually be something that disconnects and overwhelms the practitioner from casting effective magic. I actively encourage the reader to have a look at some of the tools mentioned and find what works for you.

Altar

The altar is a central and focal point for the witch, particularly when working indoors. It acts as a workbench for the practitioner, a place which suits a myriad of spiritual purposes such as sitting and communing with various spirits such as familiars or ancestors and giving them various offerings, such as performing the Houzle. Spells, charms, and divinations are also performed there as well as oils, powders, and incense made up for workings. Lastly meditation, trance work, and spirit flight or fetch flight are performed at the altar acting as a focal point for the crafters sullen arte.

Within Traditional Witchcraft the altar isn't a sacred space as such, but more of a workbench for their craft. However, within my own personal beliefs I don't feel the altar is much of sacred space, but it becomes over time more of a place of power absorbing all different energies raised with previous workings performed. You do not have to own an altar in order to practice witchcraft, I know of many witches themselves that do not own an altar as there normally tends to be so many witchcraft items they often say: well, the whole house is an altar! However, the house doesn't need to be fully kitted out in witch décor in the absence of an altar. Over the years I have had different altars and places of power I work with, at the very moment were typing this I have an altar that I use on a bread bin! This is used as needed and I take it out and do the work I need to do around it. In the future, that will change, but currently, it serves its purpose and works for me and my practice.

You can put whatever you want onto your altar, it's your altar and so your choice. No dictatorship plays a part within this. However, for those stuck, I think it important to give a basic altar layout that I not only use myself but one that I have also seen with other practitioners of the old faith. On either side of the altar, sit the two working candles as a means to offer fire to any familiar or ancestral spirits. Between the two candles at the far back of the space, sits the skull which is normally the skull of an animal in order to represent the Aulde one himself or sometimes The Mighty Dead. In front of these items can be various tools that you utilise a lot within your craft, there is also normally a spirit house of a working familiar spirit there also which aids your craft. At the foot of the altar are any large cauldrons that you may have and own. Last but not least, the stang sits behind the whole altar acting once again as a focal point to the work at hand and becoming a bridge and an Axis Mundi to the spirit world.

The Stang and the Axis Mundi

One of the most prominently featured tools within the Traditional Witch Cult is that of the stang. The stang is traditionally a forked staff of ash wood, that is shod at the bottom with an iron nail. However, within different Traditional Witch covens, stangs may differ entirely from this and are made from various kinds of wood such as hazel or blackthorn, and even feature a variety of decorative and spirit-influenced items such as an iron topper, antlers, hag stones, etc. The forked top represents the horns of the Old One and sometimes a candle is fixed between its split representing and bearing the famed witch quote: *the truth lies betwixt the horns*. The candle in the central split represents the primordial witch fire Aulde Hornie holds within him, that we ourselves carry within us also. This tool also represents what's known as an 'Axis Mundi' which translates as world tree. Traditional Witchcraft is a spiritistic tradition meaning it's a tradition that bases heavily on the influence of the spirit world. What's interesting in a lot of spiritistic traditions we tend to see the symbology of the tree playing its part acting as a medium or a totem pole. That symbolism of the tree acts as a vehicle for the spirits to travel through and become linked from the invisible world to the mundane.

For this reason and this alone, the stang becomes the main working altar when outside during ritual. It is normally used to delineate and lay the compass round with its forked top which 'pins down' the energy and afterward, is traditionally placed in the north point of the compass round acting as a Bridgeway once again between the spirit worlds. The stangs use of ritual in witchcraft was made popular primarily from the Clan of Tubal Cain and Robert Cochrane's influence. Note the words 'made popular' rather than it originates from the Clan of Tubal Cain. The stang and its associations with the witch and its use in the craft have stretched back further and longer than the 1960s, even Cecil Williamson made mention of what's known as the talking stick. The exercise given by Cecil, would involve the practitioner resting the stang by their face, in order to bring what he labelled as 'Telaesthesia' ultimately meaning the perception of future occurrences and objects without the sense of the normally recognised sense organs. In other words utilising the 'pulse spots' or the energy contained in the land, in order to facilitate psychic visions of the future.

The stang and witches are seen in older artwork such as Ulrich Molitor's *De Lamiis* in 1489 which depicts three animal-headed witches taking flight. Another is seen in the artwork known as The witches by William Edward frost in the 1800s which depicts three old witches around the fire inspired by the play Macbeth written by William Shakespeare. An additional piece of artwork which is a woodcarving made by Hans Baldung in 1510 portrays a group of witches with stangs on the floor, as well as a witch mounted upon her stang in flight, so it is something that is seen within history and there have been some associations with witches and stangs. The stang and its symbology of the world tree is one of the most important tools in the Traditional Witch Cult, as it is effectively a portable altar and medium to the Otherworld.

However, a word of controversy but I'm going to have to say it. I'm a Traditional Witch and I've over twenty years' experience and I don't use a stang during my rituals. I used to, but when you've grown up and lived in a city and never drove your whole entire life it is actually much harder to venture outdoors with a stang. The constant probing of questions not only becomes tiresome, but the attention it draws, in general, isn't really what's needed to venture to a nature reserve whilst trying to go unnoticed. For me, it drew unnecessary attention and detracted within ritual space and actually at times created moments of fear through others following me and being curious and that is NOT something you need at nine in the evening. The issue of practicality when it comes to the stang is never spoken about and so I think we need to now have the stang talk.

For a witch living in the city that doesn't drive and takes public transport to a ritual site, it can become such a detraction rather than a connection. I've had people drunk trying to steal it off me too on the bus, and even been called Gandalf (I have to admit, I was amused myself by that statement.) The point is, the stang isn't for everybody and just because it's not suited for every Old Craft practitioner doesn't mean they haven't got access to the world tree and are unable to utilise its symbolism. The world tree isn't just accessed by those with a stang and can be replaced by working with an actual tree that becomes the Axis Mundi.

However, if a tree isn't there to access then a witch can also envision the world tree within their ritual going through the compass round and acting as a gateway between spirits and man. The same goes when one lays a compass round with the absence of a stang, it can be laid with the left foot dragging along, or fingers directed around the witch rings edge. When it comes to accessing the world tree, I personally use a bull roarer instead. For me, it's so much more discreet and just generally practical. Instead of walking around Glasgow city centre like something from lord of the rings and telling buses they shalt not pass, I just put my bullroarer in my bag, off I venture to my working site, and nobody knows. I have worked with my stang outdoors and worked it during rituals that have been potent and powerful but the exact same has been done with a bullroarer. To some, this may be a bit controversial or even shocking, but I have to be honest that for me practicing my own personal craft is what works for me.

If you've not a clue what a bull roarer is don't worry, il describe it in the next part. The stang, however, still can be utilised by those within the city, the preference of the bullroarer is just my personal preference. If you are wanting a stang but are not wanting to draw attention to yourself, then a good way to still have and employ it within your rites is a 'mini stang'. Which is effectively a forked wand that you can carry in your bag, the size of it can vary to your choice but mostly I've seen it in different forms, from the forearm or to the length of the leg. The smaller stang can be carried more discreetly in the practitioner's bag en route to ritual working sites.

Many will ask, how does one acquire the stang? Well for myself in the past I have asked for one that's suitable for my practice to reveal itself to me. The entity to ask this question is none other than the horned one as the stang is a representation of himself. The ritual will take a whole day to acquire a stang, but essentially the seeker of the stang will venture out into the woods and before going into the woods will make an offering at the entry point of the place along with a small prayer to the Aulde one that is fitting for the person and their practice. I'll give an example of this but for a practitioner whose looking for the stang it is YOUR stang you're asking for and with this in mind, I think it would be best for the witch themselves to come up with their own supplication to the Aulde one:

"Lord of the wildwood, great witch master I give you this offering and supplication and I ask that in return you grant me a working stang, A forked staff to act as an Axis Mundia world tree between the world of men and the world of

spirits. A forked staff that will represent your influence power over my rituals, lord of the wildwood, old Devil of the trees and woodlands, hear my call and please grant my request."

Be specific though! If it is a smaller stang then ask! The same applies vice versa too. The first time I performed this small ritual was in Alderley Edge, Cheshire. Where there is a patch of small woodlands and then the main woodlands leading into the forest. I had performed the prior rite in the small woodlands at the first entrance way and the moment I had done the ritual, I had this feeling that the stang would be at another entrance point towards the woods. As I got towards the second entrance, the sun shone brightly upon the entrance and there right in front of me was a beautiful, forked staff that had been dug into the middle of the clearing. The light was shining onto it and with that, I took it and knew that it had been given to me, I took the moment to thank the Aulde One (which is incredibly important). The stang may not come to you this exact way, as everybody's practice is different your stang may be given differently to you.

You may be put in situations where you will need to cut a stang from the tree itself. There may even be cases where the Horned master will test you almost saying to you: "How bad do you want it?" It will come in different ways, so bring a knife just in case you're put in a position where you will need to gather it from a tree. In which case, make sure to spend time with that tree asking it if it is ok to gather its wood and give an offering back to the spirit.

Once the stang has been received and you are home then it is time to decorate it in any way you feel will work for you, some will use pyrography pens in order to score symbols integral to their craft into the working stang. Some will also carve signs but what I will say, be sure to have a piece of wood to practice on beforehand. I always find it important to make sure these are symbols you're able to have time to practice, before possibly damaging your stang.

You don't have to carve or burn symbols into your stang, again it is your practice, your craft, and above all your stang. Always make sure to treat the wood, giving it a coating of linseed oil and leaving it for two weeks to soak in the oil, then another coating of linseed oil. Two weeks after that, A final rubbing of bee's wax to seal the oils in will then help to preserve the wood of the stang. You can also decorate the stang with different items such as animal parts you associate with a familiar spirit, with the famous holed hag stones, feathers, antlers, witches' ladders, etc. The choice is entirely yours to make. You can go as simplistic or eccentric as you want.

The World Tree Ritual

Ways in which one can work with the stang as an Axis Mundi can be done differently. I feel like there are a lot of books mentioning the stang but not a lot of them go into how to access the stang itself as a world tree, which is in no way an insult to anybody I just feel it would be good for beginners to be aware of. So, bearing in mind, I'm going to take the opportunity to give an example.

The first is visualisation which can be seen in the section that goes into laying a compass round. The witch places the stang in the northward direction and thrusts it into the ground (or a bucket of sand/soil if indoors) and then precedes to hold onto the stang itself, seeing the stang grow in size larger and larger until it is incredibly large. From then on, the forked top starts to branch off into tree limbs that reach into the heavens stretching higher and higher. The middle section of the stang thickens to that of a tree trunk. The bottom part of the stang starts to sprout into roots, roots that spread into the depths of the underworld going deeper and deeper, stretching into the very core of the earth itself.

Take your time with this, visualise and see this tree forming, and hear it, hear the branches in the wind bouncing off one another, hear the roots in the depths of Elphame cracking, creaking, and the earth moving. This is no longer a stang, this has become a world tree, an Axis Mundi itself that bridges the worlds together. The stang has become a medium between the realms of men and spirits. It is in this case the practitioner will state:

"Stang/tree, be thou a bridge between heaven and hell, a gateway and sacred medium into the world of men and of spirits. From the top of the tree to the bottom of the roots, connect me to the spirit world and allow them to travel through this stang/tree as an Axis Mundi. By leaf, by twisting limb, by branch, by root, by will, be thou hollowed!"

In the absence of the working stang as mentioned, it is possible to work with and incorporate the Axis Mundi into your rites. Another way to do this ritual without the stang, is effectively by working with a tree within the working ground of the witch. Essentially, the entire ritual stays the same but instead of a stang, with a tree incorporating that as a means to call the spirits and an Axis Mundi. If any working altar items or tools for spells are needed, then they are placed at the foot of the tree, as the same with the stang itself.

In the tradition of the Cultus Sabbati or what's known as 'Sabbatic witchcraft' they make use of a tree or stang that itself acts as an Axis Mundi. Mentioned in the grimoire Azoetia by Andrew Chumbley 'the fetish tree' is known as a phallic symbol and within the circle of arte acts as an Axis Mundi world pillar that ascends to the north star. It can also be an ash pole that has signs carved upon it as well as decorations added onto it which may represent any spirits or totems of that working group.

The Bull-Roarer or Wind Roarer

I first came across this working tool when watching a fabulous open university video on YouTube of village witch Cassandra Latham demonstrating the workings that she performed for one of her clients. If anybody wants to watch this, please check it out as it's not only a fantastic video but its inspiring in a practical and down-to-earth manner. The bull-roarer is described in the museum of witchcraft by Cecil Williamson as a way a west country witch would draw in spirit forces whilst working in the countryside. By the wailing and sound it made, so much in fact he quoted:*"little wonder that the spirits would come flocking to see what all the ghastly moaning is about!'*

As mentioned by Cecil, the bull roarer, or 'wind roarer' as it is sometimes known, is a tool that creates a wailing sound, the only way to describe it is like a humming wind almost. The bullroarer is used and worked for not only calling up spirits, but also used for conjuring up winds and weather-related magic too. Alongside this, the bull roarer can also be used for working a spell and other acts of magic. Now, I mentioned in the text of the stang how the bull-roarer I used as an acting Axis Mundi, and many people may be confused by how I go about performing such a method but don't worry il teach you how.

Many will ask how the wind roarer itself isn't a forked branch, but rather than it being rigid it is fluent and can move anywhere so it can access different realms of spirits and is flexible and fluid in that sense. I want to start off I don't fully lay a compass normally when doing this, as the compass is used for going to the spirit world whereas the bullroarer is used for calling and conjuring up the spirits or drawing their attention if we want to get more specific.

I start to whirl the bullroarer by my side and envision a beautiful tree within the space I'm working in. A tree that stretches up into the stars of heaven and into the deep roots of hell. This tree becomes something other and something different. It is a medium, a channel, for the world of spirits and the world of men, and from this tree, the spirits can come through to you and vice versa, it works both ways. Now once you have this strong image in your head, raise the whirling wind roarer above you and call the spirits anyways you want such as the famous charm of calling the spirits spoken by the mother of modern witchcraft Doreen Valiente:

"Black spirits, white spirits, red spirits, grey
Come ye come ye come what may
Around and around
Throughout and about all good come running in, all ill keep out!"

Interestingly, famed play write William Shakespeare in his production of macbeth, incorporates the use of this charm within the scene concerning the witches by Hecate:

> *"Black spirits and white, red spirits and grey,*
> *Mingle, mingle, mingle, you that mingle may.*
> *Titty, Tiffin, keep it stiff in.*
> *Firedrake, Puckey, make it lucky.*
> *Liard, Robin, you must bob in.*
> *Round, around, around, about, about,*
> *All ill come running in, all good keep out."*

A mention of White, black, red and grey spirits is seen in reginald Scots discoverie of witchcraft. Which many believe Shakespeare took from sources of magical praxis at the time to accurately give detail to his play Macbeth.

Origins aside, always be sure to pour the spirits a lovely libation or lay down an offering as always to welcome them into the space you're working within.

The Bowl

The working bowl can be made of wood, China, bone, or stone and is used in the Old Craft current to give offerings to the spirits or any Gods you're working with such as holding bread or other food offerings for a ritual. It is also used to hold any powder or incense blends the practitioner is creating. It can be used as a way to hold any newly made charms that are left overnight to 'cook' in power, on top of this, it can be used to hold any waters that the practitioner is utilising in their conjurations and charms. Last but not least and on a grizzlier level the bowl can be used to hold any bodily fluids such as blood/menstrual blood as offerings or for workings, urine to scry in for detecting if a client has been bewitched, or any collected sexual fluids being the 'life force' for charms, spells, and workings.

Mortar and Pestle

Mortar and pestles are BRILLIANT and it is in my opinion that every witch needs one! They are used to primarily grind herbs for cooking usage. However, I use them to grind herbs, bones, earth, and resins down when making incense and powders. Whilst I do this depending on the actual purpose of the powders made, I go clockwise for good intentions and widdershins for more protective or sinister intentions, and the whole time I'm doing this, I allow myself to go into a light trance keeping focus on the task at hand.

The mortar and pestle can act as a way in which energy is directed directly into powders and incense. It is such a practical tool to have to hand and I've seen grinding materials down to a powder done in different ways aside from a mortar and pestle, such as using a millstone and grinding down corn whilst focusing on the intentions. I often find these tools from a practical perspective in terms of concocting different powders so incredible and efficient.

The Knife

Unlike the athame of traditional Wicca, the knife in Traditional Witchcraft the majority of the time is used as a practical tool and it does exactly what it says on the tin: it cuts. It is used for cutting herbs, cords, fabrics, drawing blood etc the list goes on. I've mentioned this before, but the knife is used for a myriad of purposes in terms of practicality when it comes to the craft. I've even used my knife to drunkenly flip burgers post ritual! It can be used as a way to direct energy but for the most part, the knife within Traditional Craft acts as a functioning 'working blade'. Some people will only work with a knife if it has been only made by themselves and forged themselves. Such an idea is brilliant and for the sake of authenticity id love to say I have crafted mine from scratch but unfortunately, I haven't ever had the opportunity arise. In all honesty, the fact that I haven't created the blade myself hasn't affected the actual working conditions and flow of the blade magically at all.

The Skull

The skull tends to be a tool that is a central focal point to the witch's altar, particularly within the witch's threshold. In some cases, it can be human but for most crafters that haven't got access to human remains an animal skull is used as a representation of The Mighty Dead. According to Nigel Jackson in his book masks of misrule, bone is seen by the Traditional Witch as a representation of crystalised spirit in its purest form, especially being the skull of an animal or human was considered the seat of the soul by the ancient Celtic tribes. The skull is also usually worked in Traditional Witchcraft rituals of tapping the bone.

The skull not only represents the link the witch has to the ancestors but also to that of Aulde Hornie, the master of witches and so the skull is put as a central point of the altar as a way for the practitioner to connect with the Aulde One, petitioning him, and working with the skull in idolatrous ways to commune with him and The Mighty Dead. We see a couple of references in history to the witches' skulls being utilised also, one of working with monkey skulls. Nowadays, many know that acquiring such a skull through the animal being killed purely for its skull is completely and utterly cruel and uncalled for. Alongside this, some monkeys are actually endangered so please think as of where the ethics behind gaining a monkey skull lie. According to Cecil Williamson:

'Witches regard monkeys as being spirits in human form. So in the southwest, it is no surprise to find monkey skulls stored away in witches' trunks and used in magic making.'

He goes on to mention monkey skulls that *'once belonged to a Kingsbridge witch called Kitty Dunn or Nunn, obtained from an antiquarian who acquired them in 1913 together with various other animal remains – teeth, tusks and polished bones.'*
Another excerpt by Cecil Williamson on the use of skulls within the arte recalls a ram's skull which appeared on a rock

shrine which was used by a group of witches up on the cliffs of Bodmin Moor. He mentions that the shrine was dismantled in 1967 after which, the last of the trio of strange women had sadly passed away.

Different Stones in Traditional Craft

The Hearthstone is a flat piece of stone that tends to sit central to the altar and is used in the unfortunate absence of a witch's hearth. It is used for drawing symbols on with chalk, for burning candles, for burning petitions or items of power, and also used as a way for the witch to make oaths or pacts with the witch Gods or spirits normally by sealing the deal via blood. Another stone that acts as a focal point as well as having several other uses for Traditional Witch rites such as in the Sabbatic craft, mentioned in Azoetia is a tool known as the God stone which is symbolic of the Penis of the horned God and is typically larger than a human phallus. The rites of hollowing it is interesting as it calls for this to be hallowed at noon by all the male members of the cult, who make an offering to it of their own life force in order to bestow it with power and virtue.

I have seen people work the latter stone alongside a holed stone also known as a hag stone. The God and Hag stone also known crudely as a 'cock and fanny' stone are conjoined together in acts of love and fertility magic. Alongside this, I've seen two different sets of stones used acting as a 'cock and arse' stone to conjoin them both in acts of gay love magic. As well as this, I've also seen two 'Fanny stones' tied together for lesbian women too. This is merely scratching the surface when we come to discuss stones, particularly within folk magic, as there is such a vast amount of different working stones when it comes to working practical folk magic too such as fairy stones, Devils thunderstones, hag stones, etc.

The Cauldron

Firstly, it is representative of the womb of Dame fate, the fiery creatrix of all and so this is symbolic of the womb of creation, and so it is with this in mind that items of power particularly newly made charms and fetishes of spirit force can be left in overnight and once the lid of the cauldron is taken off, the item emerges thus representing the fetish being 'birthed' into the mundane world.

As well as this, the cauldron itself was and still is used within some cultures for cooking up food. This is exactly the same in witchcraft in the sense that spell work can be 'cooked up' by the practitioner. The cauldron is a great vessel for containing power and energy and so the witch can also cast powerful magic within this vessel creating a vortex of their energy with intention in the cauldron with a singular lit candle.

The exercise is extremely simplistic in nature, and takes influence from Orion Foxwoods book The Flame in the Cauldron. Place a small taper candle inside the cauldron making sure its firmly stuck at the bottom and won't fall over. The witch places their hands over the side of the mouth of the cauldron giving it room for the flame of the candle to breath and ensuring you're not burning your hands. From that point, keep your complete and utter focus on the desire at hand.

See and envision your witch power coming from your hands and into the vessel. Keep pushing and directing energy into the cauldron, keeping constantly mindful of the intentions that they have, pushing into it ever more their witch power into it encompassing the lit candle within. A simplistic chant of your intention can be used alongside this action clearly stating your intentions such as:

"Healing, healing, Brian be healed"

As this is said pushing into it evermore your own power with that intention, you will eventually begin to feel pressure almost as if the pressure on the edge of the cauldron is about to pop. At this point, just leave the candle to burn down. This is simplistic but incredibly effective.

Another large purpose of the cauldron is that again it acts as a replacement for the witch's hearth in terms of burning items. Stick effigies, petitions, psalms, and incense can all be burnt within the cauldron too as a method for working fire-safe magic. I've even seen covines actually brew cider or warm ales in this cauldron and delegating it out amongst covine members and the spirits, I've even seen and had a delicious stew made in one in the middle of the woods with an Old Craft covine.

The Wand and Blasting Rod

The wand within witchcraft is something that's used and worked with as an extension of the magician's will. Typically, wands can be made of any type of wood that you feel connected towards and also from what virtues you're desiring here. It's always important to ask an actual tree for the wood before taking a piece and utilising it as a wand, in order to avoid any ill-mannered or harassed spirits on your back. Always ask and give an offering when taking some wood from a tree to collect your wand. Typically, in length, a wand is the size of a witch's forearm, however, wands can be larger or kept in a smaller 'keppen' size which is effectively a smaller wand used by the wise.

Different woods as mentioned may carry different properties with them. Another aspect of the wand in a more sinister light, is that of the blasting rod. This is something that historically has brought many people fear of various practitioners over the years, as it wasn't uncommon back in the day for cunning folk or wise women to carry a cane of some sort or a staff. Most commonly this object they carried with them brought intrigue but also fear and was sometimes known as 'the blasting rod'.

This is an item that has been found in historical practitioners such as the one carried by Essex cunning man George Pickingill whom many would be fearful over and the power, he held over folk. The blasting rod is made from the blackthorn bush, this shrub is used and worked with in the arte in order to bring affliction, illness, distraught and general workings of baneful and negative influence upon a victim of the witches target.

However, one of the other aspects of the blackthorn's virtues especially regarding its fierce and harmful thorns is that of protection and guarding qualities. These thorns have also been employed and sometimes placed into witch bottles and other workings of folk magic, as a means to protect and defend the practitioner from any malefic influences sent their way.

The Balefire

Within the central point of the compass round, lies what's known as 'the balefire' or 'the hearth fire'. This is essentially a bonfire dedicated to various entities within the operations of the witch. Many will dedicate this fire to the spirits of the land which is a good point of call, especially when working outdoors in the woods.

This will almost (but not all the time, depending on the spirit) ensure them working in your favour granted by the spirits. Another popular method is to dedicate the balefire to Old fate, the fiery creatrix of all representing the witch fire from the beginning of creation.

Lighting the fire 'in the Devil's name' ensures his watching and pervading presence over your workings bringing his powers to the ritual. However, some may light the balefire for their ancestors or familiar spirits too it entirely depends on the practices performed and the time of year. For instance, during the summer and winter solstice, I light the balefire in the name and honour of the sun marking the wheel of the year once again.

The balefire not only becomes during ritual a fire dedicated to a deity or spirit, but it, in fact, becomes a doorway into the Otherworld. Especially if were treading the mill and working the fire as a focal point within the compass round. It not only becomes a doorway between the world of men and spirits but through the rite of treading the mill, it becomes an access point to divinity itself connecting and aligning the practitioner to the light of Godhead. For indoor rituals, the hearth itself is used and worked with as an access point, but in the absence of the witch's fireplace, a working candle or the hood lamp is employed.

The Hood Lamp

A hood lamp is a device that is utilised within the Witch Cult to facilitate the ideology and symbology of the term: *the truth lies betwixt the horns*. It is either one of two things; normally a horseshoe affixed on top of a wooden block, or a small wooden pole/stick that has in between the horseshoe a candle holder or a small pin so that tapers can be affixed on top of it.

Another variation is that of blackthorn or white thorn, however, the hood lamp can be used to work effective candle magic too. It is normally employed with the candle and pins spell which is documented in the museum of witchcraft and magic in Boscastle. I have seen some crafters employ the use of the whitethorn hood lamp to work more beneficial magic such as healing, and the blackthorn hood lamp is utilised to work darker aspects of magic such as blasting, protection, shielding, and binding.

When candle magic is worked in the hood lamp, we're not only placing it betwixt a Traditional Witch tool, but it's a symbolism that we are placing the spell work in the Aulde One's name, not just putting the spell work with him, were placing it right between his horns where the source of all magic originates from. Many may wonder where the origins of the hood lamp actually arise from and what's interesting is that there isn't really a conversation to show how old this is or its origins.

Originally, the hood lamp has its origins via Kord Bucca, a working group of witches within Cornwall alongside well-known author Gemma Gary. The first image of the lamp is of what appeared on the website Cornish witchcraft. It later featured in Gemma Garys work Traditional Witchcraft: a Cornish book of ways. The term being coined by Gemma herself, hence the name 'Hood' meaning bewitched.

What's interesting, is that through history there are also some items that bear a similar resemblance. An example of this, is found in the museum of witchcraft portraying a tool used for detecting treasure found within a French book known as secrets merveilleux de la magic naturelle et cabbalistic du petit Albert. This translates to the title: the marvellous secrets of the natural and cabbalistic magic of Little Albert.

The tool itself stands between a cut piece of forked wood, in which the candle that stands is made grotesquely of human tallow. It reads as such:

'You must have a big candle composed of human tallow and it must be fixed into a forked piece of hazel wood. Then if this candle, being lighted in a subterranean place, sparkles brightly with a good deal of noise it is a sign that there is treasure in that place, and the nearer you approach the treasure then the more will the candle sparkle, going out at length when you are quite close. You must have other candles in lanterns so as not to be left in the dark."

Cecil Williamson also mentions another strange candle set between forked wood bearing a circular wire ring which resembled a cobweb-like structure, was utilised by a witch who lived at Okehampton and who used to prowl the graveyards in the dead of night.

He goes onto mention that in the south-west, there is a prevalent belief in spirits being moths, which worked well for the witch holding the contraption in the cemetery at night. As the moth become entrapped within the cobweb structure, it gave her more time to converse with the spirits of the dead. The contraption was said to have been found several years after her death concealed in a surface tomb with a loose side panel.

The Cord

The cord is a tool used within the Witch Cult for a myriad of purposes, firstly let's take a look into the symbolism of this tool and what that means for the practitioner. The cord itself represents the umbilical cord we each have that connects us to Dame fate or the Great goddess herself. This shows our link to her as our birthing mother but also it portrays the complete other side and represents the garrot or what's known as 'the hanging rope' being symbolic of death. This represents the ties we have to the cruel mother herself. From her, we are birthed by her will, and from her, we 'come home again' under her guise and under her will.

The cord in its essence represents our birth, life, and death as a whole, it represents our personal thread of fate. As well as our own, it represents others' fates and because of that we can use it to affect somebody's thread of fate whether that be for good or for ill, it is entirely our choice we make. We can use it in acts of magic via creating knots as we focus deep and intently on our intentions and with each knot made, we speak the following words as the famous knot spell goes in its different forms:

> *Knot of one spells begun,*
> *Knot of two it cometh true*
> *Knot of three, for it shall be*
> *Knot of four the power I store*
> *Knot of five the spell is alive*
> *Knot of six the spell is fixed*
> *Knot of seven by hell and heaven*
> *Knot of eight for it is fate*
> *Knot of nine, what's done is mine*

The cord is then kept in its nine knots until the working is made manifest. A practitioner can also add feathers into the cord which correspond with your working, making it into a temporary witch's ladder. In mastering witchcraft, Paul Huson writes how the cord is used to delineate and mark out a circle during ritual. The cord can also be used as a way to knot and trap in the wind and then released when required just as the witches of Boscastle used to do when selling the wind to sailors.

Thunderstorms are considered incredibly sacred to witches, and so when it thunders and lightening is present in the sky, some witches will 'knot in' the storm and release it when next needed. The energy trapped within knotted thunderstorms can be undone and ritually 'rung out' into spells, unknotting the cord blowing through the rope into the working performed at the time, and then with the hand running down the rope and flicking into the working all the energy stored. Exactly the same can be done on the full moon and harvesting the powers of the lunar powers gathered.

The witches cord can be worked in meditations either knotted or inputted with feathers and used almost as a rosary or mandala beads, either counting the chants used to help aid the practitioner in a trance-like state or using it as a way to keep focus during meditations and trance workings. When making a witch's cord, I firstly gather three pieces of thick white rope (you choose your colour, again it's YOUR cord nobody else's) and under the light of the full moon, start to plait the actual cord itself creating a thicker rope.

Allow yourself to go back and forth into a trance-like state, once this is done and the cord is bound on both sides, so it won't unwind. Then keep your eyes affixed upon the full moon, creating an open loop that you're able to look through and keep your gaze at the moon, then once this has been done tightly pull trapping some of the moon's energy into that. Do this nine times evenly keeping the knots in the cord and then leave it out overnight to charge in the light of the full moon. After this, your cord has been hallowed and ready to use in the ways that serve you.

When Tools No Longer Serve You

There will come a point and time within your personal praxis that you may outgrow tools, or that they will not become as needed or needed at all as they did in the first years of practice. This is absolutely ok, it shows growth and development which is a great thing! The tools are there to help us within our craft that is why they are called tools. However, all being said witchcraft is an animistic practice and so with the idea of natural items having spirits or essences the exact same goes for the tools.

So yes, they can help and assist you, and that is what they are for but having used and worked with your tools for years they will have their own spirit. Not only this, but essentially just think of all the power you would have raised through working with them for years, that's a lot of energy that those tools will hold.

The following ritual is designed so that the practitioner could give back to the land and say a final farewell to previous working tools. A lot of books we see have instructions for gaining tools, but there isn't really a ritual that helps us say goodbye to our tools if we've moved forward in our practice and they are no longer needed.

Now, don't get me wrong I know people that have had their trusted stang for years and years and do not at any point desire to let go of it. That is absolutely fine, but people are different and so is their practice. In the instance of me earlier regarding the stang I don't use a stang and it came to a point they were just sitting and gathering up dust.

The basis for this ritual is ancient and an incredibly old ritual itself, it is not word from word or action from action but the overall act itself is based on the following: It has been found, that the ancients of Britain particularly the celts left votive offerings at bodies of water. Quite often, this would be metal work such as swords or daggers and they would be broken in two.

The idea behind this that some archaeologists have had, is that by breaking the dagger in two it is a symbolism that the power of the dagger is no longer used for the mundane world around us. Rather than, it has been given over to the spirit world as an offering for their use.

That's exactly what you're doing in this small rite, you're given this tool that you've had a working relationship with for years and welded all this energy and had all these experiences with and giving it to the spirit world. This is a big sacrifice. Especially if this is a place you work regularly within, to the spirits of the land it's a massive offering.

The Ritual

To start off with, a couple of days prior sit down with the tool in front of you in a place where you will not be interrupted at all. Make time for this tool, just as you would make time to have a serious conversation with an old friend. After all, you're essentially going to be severing ties with this tool.

Sit crossed-legged and take ten deep breaths, clearing your mind from mundane instances and allowing your mind to become clear. After these deep cleansing breaths have been taken, start to focus on your tool in front of you. Notice any patterns, any groves you've not seen before, and really sit and observe this keeping a deep focus on the physical aspect of the tool and remember to really take your time with this.

After this has been done, take the tool with both hands and close your eyes and take yourself through a timeline of the tool's life. See the moment yourself and the tool first 'met' start to take yourself through a timeline of the tool's life, think back to rituals you've both been included in and how you've used your tool, try to keep focus, on any memories you have of the tool spiritual or even mundane.

Did you stang help you through a large hiking trip you took? Has your wand assisted in a spell that was so effective? Try to think back and keep those memories alive. Really take your time with this, now open your eyes slowly and place your tool in front of you again and start to see its spirit. That's right visualise its spirit, see the spirit of that object coming out of the tool, see its traits, and keep that strong visualisation.

See it staring back at you, keep your witch sight going, focus on the spirit of the tool, and then start to talk to it. Start to talk to this spirit about the reason you're calling it up and mention how you feel that the tool itself is no longer needed but be appreciative.

Tell this spirit how it helped you in huge ways and that you wouldn't be where you are in your practice without its help and assistance, tell it how beautiful it is, and how thankful you are but that you've reached a point in your practice now it's not needed, it's nothing personal it's just that you've progressed within your practice.

However, in doing so you are going to give the tool back to the spirit world so that it can go forward in the invisible world taking on its own form, shape and essentially having its own life, it's time to go your separate ways. As a side-note, the spirit may object and want to stay in your company and practice which case if its fine with yourself, tell the spirit it can come and live in another object or that you'll make it a spirit house but give the spirit terms and conditions.

A large term and condition are that the spirit will assist you in your practice but if the spirit does not want to budge, remind it that the tool it was attached to is no longer needed, and because it will then become a familiar spirit if it stays in your company and assists you in your practice.

It has to suit your craft and work for you which is the whole reason you're doing this ritual, but again normally the spirit won't have a problem with going over to the other side if it is no longer needed. The reason I mention this, is that I had a broom once that had an imp in it over the years that had taken residence and didn't want to budge when I performed this ritual and deals and pacts with the spirit were established and he has come along with me still playing a part to this day.

Remember to thank the spirit for the time it has served you, and the time it has added to your practice, that is an incredibly important part of this ritual. A couple of days later, go to a body of water (a river suits this fine, preferably with a bridge) and taking the tool in your hands and holding it above your head say the following or something that is similar to your own choice:

"As some is given so some is taken back, I give this tool back to the spirit world crafted from my own hands, an instrument to my sullen arte that I've had through the years that have helped me and assisted me in my practice. I give this tool back to the world of the spirits, I give it to the spirits of the land, so that it may continue its use in the world of spirits to become a powerful instrument to them. Spirits of the land, I give this to you as a sacrifice. Accept my sacrifice spirits as I say farewell dear (item) you have served me well and for that, there is no greater offering than to the world of spirits"

Break the tool in half at that point if it is a wand then snap it, if it is a stang and you're on a bridge rest it upon a ledge and snap it in half in the centre using your leg to kick it, if it is a cord, then cut it in two with a pair of scissors. After the tool has been physically broken, state the following:

"As it is physically broken, so it represents the use for it no longer being in the physical world, but its use is only now accessible in the spirit world. I give this to the world of spirits"

Throw the items in the bed of water whilst saying:

"It is done. It is done. It is done!"

Take some time to stare at the item as it is embedded into the body of water and say your final goodbye to it, the tool has served you well but has now been given back to the world of spirits. Walk away and do not at any costs, look back.

The last point to make, is if at any chance the tool has any items on it that are not going to be taken in an environmentally friendly way then perhaps take them off and dispose of them in a different way than depositing them in nature, sticks, natural twine, are all fine but for instance, nothing says dishonouring the spirits of the land like throwing in some cheeky plastic to a river! Think and make sure the votive offering you will be giving is ecologically friendly and not going to be harmful to the body of water and the inhabitants within it.

Meditation as a Means for Witchcraft

I could genuinely be able to write a book on meditation and the effect it has on a practitioner on their path of witchcraft. Not even from a perspective of a person being a witch, just from the perspective of being a human, meditation is brilliant for a person's well-being, their mindset, and goes hand in hand with health altogether. We live in such a fast-paced world now, where there are expectations, work deadlines, reminders to pay bills, and responsibilities that tie us to our physical life, where there is always something that you must do that involves something so mundane and beige.

Quite frankly we are subjected and exposed to a constant to-do list of monotonous chores to complete that most of the time throws us off from truly experiencing our lives and being in the moment. That is where Meditation comes into it, it reminds us to take that time to relax, and to be in the present. Meditation is something I've found that throughout my time, has only ever added to my life, it has never taken away and it has a ripple effect on other areas of my life and gives me a more collected outlook on life in general. It's one of those things that admittedly despite writing about it, I've not fully mastered.

It's something that I will go ages without and remember and realise how much good it brings into my life then I become militant with it, and I notice such a difference to my life in general. So, I've still not mastered it and I have a feeling il be trying to master it until the day I venture to the next life. Meditation is an eastern practice originally and so many will ask the following: How does this benefit my witchcraft practice?

When meditating, you shut out the outside world. All those mundane thoughts that constantly swamp our brains melt away. For once we get a break from that exhausting self-dialogue which can be useful but it's also something that when we're practicing magic, we need to hold within us the complete and utter focus of having the gnosis that that spell or charm were working will take effect and will work.

By keeping our minds focused for 10 minutes a day and training our brains to keep out external mundane thoughts, that come entirely useful within practicing magic and keeping our focus on the desired effect at hand. It helps sharpen our will to were wanting to drive it. Meditation is so useful when it comes down to it, not only that but it's so useful when we want to commune with the spirit world which helps us deepen our relationship with them. It lets us keep an open mind and gives them the opportunity to be heard and to be felt.

Once again it allows us to block out all the hustle and bustle of everyday life and quieten our minds keeping a relaxed and calmed mindset. Despite the amount of sheer crazy mundane stress we carry in our jobs, in our home lives, and sometimes in our social lives NO WONDER many people can't see or feel the spirit world! They're too busy!

Such a thought of all this amount of responsibility of being an adult can make one want to run away and live off-grid but explaining how frustrating day-to-day life can be is starting to come off as a rant and I can't trust myself at times, so let's get back to the subject at hand.

Meditation overall when it comes to your craft is a God send and something I enjoy doing on my day off is sitting at my altar first thing in the morning with a cup of coffee and lighting incense and meditating for 10 minutes a day. Just ten minutes, if I'm working then I'll try and attempt it when I'm back from work and as mentioned I'm no angel when it comes to this, admittedly it's something I'm not disciplined with at all.

So how does one go about meditating? Well, there is active meditation which I find very fitting, especially to those of Traditional Witchcraft and it was something I heard when meeting and talking to a Toad witch who practiced walking meditation daily. He went for a walk in the woods and kept his mind completely free and taking in the moment, being in the present with nature and that's one very simplistic but incredibly effective form of meditation.

Another is more to what somebody would associate meditation with, which is sitting at your altar or laying down making sure you're comfortable and not at all going to be interrupted. I tend to play some shamanic drumming for this or singing bowls, anything that takes my mind to a more trance-like state.

I sit at my altar crossed-legged, light my two working candles on either side of my altar and perhaps some incense, and then take deep breaths. Through the nose, and out through the mouth, deep cleansing breaths help facilitate to relax the body and clear the mind.

From this point remember to keep your mind focused on a completely blank canvas, completely blank. Random thoughts will get into your head but just learn to acknowledge them as this is completely natural to what we're constantly subjected to.

Acknowledge those thoughts and release them, don't try to fight them as this will only make those thoughts more overwhelmingly prominent. Acknowledge and release those passing thoughts. Keep this up for 10 minutes, that's all just ten minutes a day can make such a difference to yourself, your practice, and the connection and relationship you have with the spirit world. In my opinion, meditation is a brilliant method for any practitioner of the magical arts.

Plants, Herbs, and Wortcunning

Witchcraft being of an animistic belief system holds no boundaries to that of the plant world. In fact, it actively embraces them and has for a very long time. The different plants, herbs, shrubs, and trees, all carry with them different influences and powers which can be effectively worked with and brought into your own rites and spell work.

Over the many different years, these plants hold associations with them through a rich myriad of stories, lore, and tales. Each plant will not only have its own spirit, but it will indeed have its own virtues that it holds, and this is easily accessed if the person harvesting the plant approaches it in a polite, and respectful manner.

For instance, you're not going to want to pull up and uproot an entire bush just because you're wanting a couple of the plant's petals for a working? Let the plant flourish and live its best life! That plant itself acts as a biodiverse ecosystem for so many different animals and it's not only a feasible life form within itself and has the right to be here as much as you. Always ask the plant itself if you're able to work with it and explain why you're working with it! Explain what working you're doing, always ask before you take what isn't yours and it is no different with plants and herbs.

The ways of the green or wort cunning as it is known within Traditional Witchcraft, is the employment of plants and herbs in order to cause magical effect and this can be done in so many versatile ways. Plants can be sprinkled into the shoes of somebody you're wanting to influence, they can be hung up in somebody's threshold in order to bring specific influences like protections and warding, they can be inputted into talismans and charms alike, added to incenses, put into baths and waters in order to once again bring specific influences the witch is wanting.

The ways in which a person can work with herbs and plants are vastly versatile. With the aforesaid mentioned regarding different properties each plant will have, how does a person actually find out the magical properties of the plants?

Well, an activity I enjoy doing is researching the different folklore and stories attached to a plant and what it can add to a working. Folklore will hold countless associations with the natural world whether that be natural places within the landscape, megaliths, or stone circles and plants are no different at all.

An example of this could be the hawthorn bush, known as a faery tree, so much so that still to this day certain people in Ireland will build roads around those trees for fear of upsetting the good folk. Another example could be the blackthorn as mentioned prior regarding the blasting rod, the list is vast, and honestly, it's one of those ones where folklore is so rich when it comes to plants that you can honestly end up with another book regarding the plant kingdom and their virtues.

Another aspect of plant lore that comes into my mind is going back to the open university video I mentioned earlier of Cassandra Latham jones regarding working with plants within magical praxis. She states that nature gives you pretty much a good indication of what is useful for. If it's pretty, it may be used for beneficial workings such as love and if it's gnarly and a bit spiky then it's most probably used for protective workings or more negative based witchcraft.

Sometimes different plants and the way they grow or behave can really have an effect on what you're needing for instance if ivy or honeysuckle strangles or suffocates then perhaps using that as a way to bind somebody or to prohibit somebodies' harmful actions could be a great way to employ these virtues and properties. Not only that, but even after the plant itself has been cut it's doing what comes naturally to it.

Ways to also bond and connect with a plant is to grow them from seed, and start to see the process of that. It's a way in which not only do you become familiar with the plant's stages and identification, but you can spend the time studying any folklore attached to it. Also, by doing this and caring for that plant you become acquainted with its spirit and are able to be more likely at connecting to it in the future for its assistance in future workings.

Often, we can just find a plant that grabs us for a working in mind and we may sometimes not even know what it is, but we feel that we need to incorporate that plant into our conjurations or charms used. Some people may absolutely not agree with this, but honestly, do you want to know something? That is absolutely alright! Nothing is wrong with being guided by the spirits to input a plant or herb into your working. Always as a precautionary, however, use gloves as some of these plants can be contact poisons which is not a situation you would want to get yourself in at all! Be very careful when working with plants and herbs.

Another aspect is that plants and herbs can be utilised for their medical purposes such as making tinctures, or teas in order to cure any sundry ailments a person may have. For instance, the elderflower and elderberry can be made into a tincture that is absolutely GREAT for cold and flu season, and making a tincture is such an easy process.

However, once again always make sure you have the correct identification of the plant itself. Be absolutely certain that what you're working with is the correct plant, because there are some plants that look alike which can be fatal such as the flowers on hemlock waterdrop compared to the elderflowers. Sadly, there have been stories where a misidentification has resulted in the hospital or even worse, so without scaring you absolutely silly and putting the fear of the Gods into you, by Christ just make sure you're absolutely certain!

Wort Cunning Charm Of Farey Hare

Believe it or not, not all plants have folklore attached to them. Sometimes this can leave us feeling a bit unsure as to what to work with that specific plant for. Perhaps we feel a pull towards that plant. Maybe something deep inside us or the spirits with which we're working with, have called us to work with that plant? Always go by your gut when such things arise and listen to your spirits and your instincts.

Of course, please do not get me wrong. It's important to look into folklore and research those plants needed but it's also important sometimes, especially when it comes to the craft to go by your gut and use your instinct. Because of this, my gorgeous cousin (yes, there's more than one witch in our family) came up with this simplistic but effective exercise where you take that time to commune with the spirit of that plant and it is YOU that asks them what their purpose is for.

Obviously, try and get the plant's actual identification on things first and foremost, and then sit down on the floor keeping cross-legged and start to clour your mind taking deep in-breaths and out-breaths. Take your time and just start to meditate with the plant, hold the plant and ask it the following: *"what are you for magically?"* just take that time and sit down keeping a clear mind, keep very calm, and await a reply.

The first thing to come into your head will be the answer or connection to that answer. After this is done, take time also to thank that plant, the spirit of the plant has made that effort to come to you after all!

The Wheel

Often, in many books based around Old Craft and just witchcraft in general, we will have what normally entails a whole chapter dedicated to the festivals or what some have come to know as 'High days' or 'Sabbats'. Before going into the sabbats themselves, I want to point out that first and foremost, I'm not going to be dedicating a whole entire chapter or a large portion of this book towards the sabbats.

The reason being, that it has been done many times before and including a large vast of knowledge regarding the sabbats for the reader will seem pointless. I think when it comes down to it, there are so many books that go into them so incredibly well and have mentioned many key points we know that needs to be made aware regarding the high days within witchcraft.

That's not a read or a slate to those books that do this as such books are incredibly useful. I just feel for this book, it doesn't seem relevant to go as in-depth as previous books have done. Regarding the sabbats, these typical high days we see in the old faith are known as Winter solstice, Imbolc/The Quickening, Beltaine, Summer solstice, Lammas, and Samhain'.

I'm going to take you through these days that are observed, typically the spring equinox and the autumnal equinox aren't days that are observed as much by those who practice Traditional Witchcraft. As they are astronomical events within themselves but aren't necessary days that have much in way of as much Pagan history compared to the other high days.

I have, however, had Traditional Witches ask me if they can practice Traditional Witchcraft, but if their still able to observe these days and the answer is YES! Of course, you are! It is absolutely your craft and your practice.

Once again you do whatever the hell you want to do in your own personal practice. It is your practice and doesn't belong to anybody else, with that in mind, let's look at some of the sabbats and the interpretation of each one:

The darkest and longest night of the year descends upon us, and winter holds its icy grip upon the land as the eve of the winter solstice looms. It is the 20th of December and Despite darkness taking the land, this is a time of promise and hope as it is from this point that with the longest night alongside the shortest day of the year, the nights will start to get shorter and the days will get longer marking the very beginning of the suns reign over the year. The lighter half of the year is in its very beginning stages, and many witches will see this as the rebirth of the Sun.

Winter solstice: let's be completely honest here, during the time of the winter solstice, it is absolutely freezing. There's going out and practicing all year round which to me is important as a practitioner as you get to mark the year properly. But despite it being the shortest night of the year, staying out all evening to greet the rising sun to myself is something that I've personally avoided as I don't drive. If I drove, then I would be venturing out but for someone in terms of practicality that doesn't drive staying out all night in snow in the UK is not only miserable, but dangerous.

For this time of year what I prefer to do, is to set up an altar the night of the solstice eve, and to light candles and incense and have some good drink and invite friends over. What's placed onto the altar is a yule log, a chunk of log in which is decorated with holly and candles. On top of this, holly, ivy, and mistletoe are all cut down, with suitable offerings given in return, and brought into the threshold to decorate the house, so that it allows the energy and powers of the land to come into the practitioner's household.

Though the land may be frozen over, it is essentially surrounding the practitioner with evergreen powers. Essentially this is like a Christmas party, but with an altar and a yule log in place in which people can place lighted tealights down onto the log for the coming year ahead. After all, this is a time of rebirth and light pervading the land once again, the lighter the better.

We come to the 2nd of February and with the days being longer, shoots of plants start to occur all around us, and plants and trees are beginning to show the very first signs of life. Vast amounts of lore are attributed to the Goddess or Saint Brighid or Bride on this day who takes ownership of the land and snowdrops are a symbol of such a thing occurring.

In fact, many say that when the snowdrops arrive is when Imbolc has descended upon the land. Not only this, but the animals around us are starting to stir and wake from hibernation. This is a time that those of the Traditional Craft will often call the 'quickening' coming from the term the 'quick' which means the living. This is also the last night of the wild hunt's reign, and after Traditional Craft rituals have been finished, we will howl to the skies as an acknowledgment of the wild hunt.

Imbolc or 'the quickening': This one can vary a wee bit here. Often, a place to go is a well or a body of water as the legends and stories of Cailleach the winter hag Goddess washing in the water and transforming into Brigid the spring Goddess who becomes the maiden of the lighter half of the year.

Another place to venture is essentially any place sacred to St Brigid or Brighid, these can vary such as an area. A sacred place such as Kilbride in Ireland that has the well of bride as well as the celebration of La Fheile Bride, which the whole town celebrates. Another place is West Kilbride in Scotland, which heavily associated with legends and lore concerning St Bride. Essentially, any pilgrimage to a sacred place concerning Brigid is often the best suitable piece of advice here.

The 1st of may falls upon the land and life is all around us! Fecundity and fertility fill the air, life is around us and the days are noticeably longer as well as lighter. The light has prevailed! It is traditional upon this day for a person to wash their face in the morning dew, for it is said to bring youth and beauty to one who performs this. Mayday is all about welcoming in the summertime and bringing in summers reign. Summer is a comin in is a traditional ballad sung during this time to welcome lifeforce within nature. A figurehead during this time worked with by some witches, is Jack in the green or the Green man being the spirit of nature. This is a time of celebration, life force, sex and it is also traditional to get drunk this time of year. Mayday or Beltaine: This is a strange one, as Beltaine and Samhain seem to be of the highest importance here as festivals being the two major Celtic fire festivals in the calendar.

However, I often have struggled in terms of getting the feel of the energy at Beltane, as it is a very physical celebration, often I find I don't get any spiritual feelings from it. It feels to me that this is something to be physically celebrated. Essentially, have sex on that day with somebody in celebration of the earth once again becoming fertile. Another aspect here is of attending any Beltaine or may day celebrations, such as the Edinburgh fire festival up on Carlton hill, the Hastings Jack in the Green festival, or any other fire festivals and Beltaine festivals.

The longest day of the year descends upon us and lifeforce and light holds its reign over the land. It is the 21st of June and despite the sun being at its zenith, this is a time that from this point the days will slowly start to get shorter and the nights longer, as the darker half of the year starts to take its grip upon the land. Eventually darkness will prevail and the summer solstice as a celebration of the sun is an acknowledgment that the days will get shorter and the nights longer. It is the very beginning stages of darkness having its grip upon the land.

Summer solstice: during the shortest night of the year, it is customary to spend the evening in a stone circle and to witness and greet the rising sun in the morning. A good idea is to venture to a stone circle and then welcome the sun in the morning.

Choose wisely however as to what stone circle you're going to venture to, as I have unfortunately been to Stonehenge and Avebury stone circle during this time and watched the land and these sacred places become absolutely trashed.

Seek out any closer and hidden stone circles in your area, I and a group of friends used to spend it in a stone circle in Alderley Edge in a place called druids circle which has many stories of witches practicing in it (particularly that of Alex Sanders coven). The stone circle itself was actually a folly and was only created in the Victorian times but in terms of energy it still had brilliant energy and power to it.

The last sheath of corn has been cut from the fields and the harvest is amongst us! The earth has given its grains, but the price of the land must be paid and sacrifice must be made. Lammas also known as Lughnasa or 'loaf mass' is a time of sacrifice. The time of august the 1st is where an effigy known as John Barleycorn who acts as the slain king actively gives himself up for the harvest of the land. And in his sacrifice becomes the sacrificial God thus becoming that of the Gods.

Lammas is a powerful time for giving back to the land to be thankful for what has been received by the land. Lammas:

within this time of sacrifice and of giving back to the earth, it is often a good time to venture to a field of corn where the very last sheath of corn has been cut from the field and a John Barleycorn is made from the actual land itself.

Another place of choosing for rituals is that of ancient burial mounds. It is a time when the burial mounds being a place of death is a great place to take your chosen and handmade John Barleycorn to get sacrificed, and his body interred into the burial mounds in order to be given back to the land under his guise as the slain god.

Another aspect of this festival is to make bread to be used as part of the Houzle ceremony at the end of the ritual, as the term Lammas comes from the term: 'loaf mass'. The john barleycorn itself can be made also from bread mix instead of the last sheath of corn, or sometimes the corn itself can be interred into the figure.

The darker half of the year is well and truly in force! A charcoal smell fills the air, the air grows crisp, and trees become a wave of deep reds, browns, and vibrant yellows as death take its hold on the land. This is Samhain, the ancient Celtic festival of the dead now known as Halloween on the 31st of October. A time for honouring the ancestors, and recognising that death takes the land and eventually it will take its grip on all living things including ourselves. It is a time to keep our ancestors in mind, as the veil between the world of the living and dead is at its thinnest and their presence is made more known.

Samhain: The most obvious place for working during the rite of Samhain and honouring the time of the dead is a cemetery at night. Even preferably a place where your ancestors rest such as their grave or their plot is something that the practitioner would benefit nicely from. Working so close in proximity to their bones, however, if there are no ancestors within the place of working then performing the ritual within a crossroads in a cemetery will suffice, but always remember to pay the 'grim' of the cemetery beforehand.

The grim is the actual guardian of that place who protects the land. This is often done but pouring a libation or throwing a coin by the entrance whilst venturing in. I often give two pence coins as an offering to this spirit, representing the two coins that were placed upon the eyes of the deseased to pay the ferryman when crossing the river Styx to the world of spirit. The burial mound once again is a place where the ancestors can be venerated by the practitioner too during this time of year.

Witch Gods: Tutelary Deities Worked on the Cunning Path

As a rule, many Traditional Witches don't actively worship the Gods, they know they exist and in doing so, may acknowledge them and may have a working relationship with them, but never really worshipping them. One of the misinterpreted delineations is that there is a large difference between worshipping and having an actively strengthened working relationship with a Diety. A relationship is essentially a trade for a trade to meet yours and the other's needs that hold deep respect, trust, and love for that entity, whereas worship is placing something higher than your own needs. Some Traditional Witches also acknowledge the Gods but might not have a working relationship with them. Placing more of their relationships with that of the ancestral dead and domestic spirits such as the familiar which seems to be quite prevalent within the faith.

The ranges of different Deities one may work within the Old Craft traditions vary, as do their origins vary drastically. Some may work with the Norse Goddess of the underworld Hel, whilst others may work with the Greek Hecate. This indicates a cross-over of different cultures and pantheons of varying belief systems including; Paganism, Christianity, and Luciferianism, making the path of Traditional Witchcraft not strictly one area. It becomes fluid, showing different influences over time that lead to the progression of the spiritual beliefs and practices we have now which I find beautiful.

Some Traditional Witches will not work at all with Pagan Gods, some will not work at all with Christian elements, it varies from practitioner. However, typically there is an acknowledgment of different belief systems blending together forming the melting pot of juxtaposition we have come to know as Traditional Witchcraft. It's impossible for me to put all of the Gods that one tends to find more prominently within

Traditional Witchcraft as each covine, group, and ultimately each individual is different. I'm going to however, include a section on various Gods/Goddesses that are found within Old Craft workings that will hold a lot of prevalence to the majority of practitioners. Once again everyone is different, but these Gods tend to be acknowledged within most folk witches practices.

Yahweh 'Jehovah' The Abrahamic Monotheistic God

Surely not you're thinking. Witches don't work with the Abrahamic God? However, il explain what this means. You see, as Traditional Witches, a lot of us will employ past and previously used spells, charms, conjurations, and other spoken and written words from history that have been supplied by popular magicians of the early modern period to the early nineteen hundreds. Cunning folk were primarily Christian at the time, and whilst they may have incorporated elements of Paganism such as working with the faery folk, or working within stone circles, primarily they were Christian and so when we perform the following famous charm from cunning folk such as curing bewitchment from Pendle witch Old Chattox, we're also petitioning the monotheistic God:

"Three biters hast thou bitten, the hart, ill eye, ill tongue: three bitter shall be thy boot, father son and the holy ghost in God's name five pater nesters five aves, and a credo in the worship of five wounds of our Lord."

Like it or not, when we perform older popish charms, were actively calling in the influence of God as were addressing the Abrahamic Deity during working older forms of praxis in folk magic. We're also doing exactly that when we work psalms too, which is something that many Traditional Witches will incorporate into their folk magic which has been used by wise men and wise women over the ages. These are all older forms of folk magic that cunning folk will employ the powers and assistance of the Abrahamic God or different aspects of God such as the incorporation of the holy trinity. Now don't get me wrong, there are many witches that don't feel comfortable at all working more Christian-based magic which is ok.

However, for the historical ties to cunning folk and their practices, it is useful to include God in this. Magical practitioners over the years, have incorporated God into their practices in ways that a conventional Christian would not deem 'acceptable' or even do themselves so it's incredibly different when we try to compare this to mainstream Christianity. For instance, Renfrewshire witch Catherine Campbell before being executed in Paisley, cursed her accusers in the name of God and the Devil. Such a statement is sad to see how desperate she was that she wanted to curse her accusers through their awful treatment of her by any means necessary, but it also emulates that magical practitioners and those termed as witches over the years didn't work with God in a conventional manner to what Christians would do.

Rather than praying to God as a Christian would do, a cunning folk or witch would work with God as a means to conjure or cause a spell. Now working with the Abrahamic God doesn't mean you can't work with other Gods or Goddesses! I do exactly this, and genuinely do my own thing. However, for the sake of argument, I think it is best to include the monotheistic Christian God in this section. If we really think about it too, Jesus Christ and the holy spirit work alongside God when we perform these older charms, as well as other saints when we again work older operations from cunning folk that incorporate the influences of saints and their assistance.

Tubal Cain and Azazel

"And Azazel taught men to make swords and knives and shields and breastplates and made known to them the metals of the earth and the art of working them; and bracelets and ornaments; and the use of antimony and the beautifying of the eyelids; and all kinds of costly stones and all colouring tinctures. And there arose much godlessness, and they

committed fornication, and they have led astray and became corrupt in all their ways."
-1 Enoch 2.8

Within the Old Craft, another aspect that holds great reverence is that of black smithery. Being the ability to shape and change metals and their forms into instruments of power. This ability of black smithery was seen by some as an act of magic in itself and in fact, there would be those who would look at blacksmiths with fear to some extent. As it was known that their art was magical and therefore, what were they capable of to others around them?

Black smithery and the otherworldly powers have always had crossovers throughout the ages, such as the European tale of the blacksmith and the Devil, in which the Blacksmith approaches the Devil wanting to make a pact for power but then tricking the Devil with his trade. The variations differ in endings as through different cultures they have been adopted.

Another interesting thing to note about black smithery is that it runs parallel to folk magic in some cases. The belief that Iron can ward away the faery folk and their intentions, it was also a deterrent against malicious magic. So much so, that James Cunning Murrell the cunning man of Hadleigh would consult the local blacksmith and have his famous witch bottles made from the iron for which he would pay the smith a shilling in doing so. In the witch trial of Allison Pearson in 1588 Scotland, we see her explain that her teacher of the craft known as William Simpson was the king's blacksmith.

Because of these many tales and different traditions of the blacksmith and his domain, there are two figureheads that hold large influence over modern Traditional Witchcraft that we have today, and these are Tubal Cain and Azazel. These two figureheads, especially in reference to Tubal Cain have their influences on Traditional Witchcraft due to Robert Cochrane and the Clan of Tubal Cain tradition of witchcraft in the 1960s. When it comes to Tubal Cain, he is first referenced in the bible (genesis 4:22) as the first blacksmith and the relative of Cain 'the first murderer'. Tubal Cain is stated in genesis as the forger 'of all instruments of bronze and iron or the instructor of every artificer in brass and iron'. It is thought, that because he was Cain's relative and because he crafted weapons that could kill and inflict harm, he invoked his ancestors sin of murder in order to do this.

In conjunction with the idea of inherited sin, we also see the incorporation of another entity with which Tubal Cain lies in similarity. It is considered that the following entity known as 'Azazel' is the more infernal aspect of Tubal Cain. Azazel originally was said to be part of a group of angels known as the watchers, that would watch over mankind. According to the book of Enoch, it was said that the angels themselves became tempted by the women with whom they found attractive and gave into their desires.

The women gave birth to a race of creatures known as the Nephilim who were said to be unusually strong Giants who lived before the great flood. Because of this conjunction between the divine and mankind, the watchers taught the women remedies of plants, enchantments, charms and astrology and in some cases these women were seen to be the first witches. Those who gained knowledge of unauthorised information and the techniques to benefit their lives with gnosis only known by Godhead and its angelic beings, but originally not meant for mankind.

Many aspects of witchcraft and magic were taught to mankind. Azazel however, was the only one to teach men to craft tools and swords from iron. What's interesting, is there really are a couple of crossovers between these two entities. In the antiquities of the Jews, Tubal Cain was said to be unusually large and strong in strength. Could he perhaps have been a Nephilim himself? Could he have been half a fallen angel? Another idea is that Tubal Cain was said to be the first blacksmith, so does that mean that Tubal Cain was the first person taught by Azazel who taught men how to forge weapons out of iron? Either way, you look at it, the link between Tubal Cain and fallen angels seems very connected.

On the Jewish day of atonement known as Yom Kippur, a day where the Israelites were to confess all their sins, two goats would be chosen for this ritual. One goat would be given to God and sacrificed at an altar, giving it as an offering to the Abrahamic Diety. The other would be pushed out into the desert for the other God known as Azazel, bearing all of the sins of the Israelite people. Hence the term we come to know as 'scapegoat'. This raises the question, is Azazel the polar God? This gruesome ritual of the past, gives the impression that 'the other God' was being appeased in order to keep him away from others. Another aspect is that of the elements and influence of freemasonry upon the Witch Cult. Within freemasonry they see Tubal Cain as one of the first forefathers of all master craftsmen, and this is something that is seen within the third-degree initiation into the masons of being able to master craft under the honour of Tubal Cain. The following is taken from a book published in 1845 known as the lexicon of freemasonry by Albert G Mackay:

...introduced many arts into the society which tended towards its improvement and civilization. Tubal Cain is the Vulcan of the Pagans and is thought to have been closely connected with ancient Freemasonry. Faber says that "all the most remarkable ancient buildings of Greece, Egypt, and Asia Minor, were ascribed to Cabirean or Cyclopean Masons," the descendants of Vulcan, Dhu Balcan, the god Balcan, or Tubal Cain. Oliver says, "In after times Tubal Cain, under the name of Vulcan and his Cyclops, figured as workers in metals and inventors of the mysteries; and hence it is probable that he was the hierophant of a similar institution in his day, copied from the previous system of Seth, and applied to the improvement of schemes more adapted to the physical pursuits of the race to which he belonged."

What's also performed in freemasonry is the special handshakes that identify a person's rank, and especially of the third degree is a handshake that represents Tubal Cain himself. On top of this, they have a specific symbol they have being two balls and a cane hence the term 'two ball cane. Interestingly enough the symbol itself looks like a backward seven, this is no mistake made or even a coincidence, as Tubal Cain was said to be the 7th generation of humans. So that's why the number seven is attributed to him. Within witch lore, however, there does also tend to be this belief that if someone is born of the seventh son of a seventh son, or if they are born the seventh person they are therefore gifted with magical ability and power.

His relative Cain the first murderer is also mentioned in the bible in particular with the number seven. As is also the story of Cain and Abel (sometimes seen as the divine twins within traditional witchcraft) the first murderer and the first sacrificed, mentioned within Genesis 4:24:

12 "When you work the ground, it will no longer yield its crops for you. You will be a restless wanderer on the earth."

13 Cain said to the LORD, "My punishment is more than I can bear."

14 "Today you are driving me from the land, and I will be hidden from your presence; I will be a restless wanderer on the earth, and whoever finds me will kill me."

15 But the LORD said to him, "Not so; anyone who kills Cain will suffer vengeance seven times over." Then the LORD put a mark on Cain so that no one who found him would kill him.

16 So Cain went out from the LORD's presence and lived in the land of Nod, east of Eden.

17 Cain made love to his wife, and she became pregnant and gave birth to Enoch. Cain was then building a city, and he named it after his son Enoch.

18 To Enoch was born Irad, and Irad was the father of Mehujael, and Mehujael was the father of Methushael, and Methushael was the father of Lamech.

19 Lamech married two women, one named Adah and the other Zillah.

20 Adah gave birth to Jabal; he was the father of those who live in tents and raise livestock.

21 His brother's name was Jubal; he was the father of all who play stringed instruments and pipes.

22 Zillah also had a son, Tubal-Cain, who forged all kinds of tools out of bronze and iron. Tubal-Cain's sister was Naamah.

23 Lamech said to his wives, "Adah and Zillah, listen to me; wives of Lamech, hear my words. I have killed a man for wounding me, a young man for injuring me."

24 "If Cain is avenged seven times, then Lamech seventy-seven times."

<u>25</u> Adam made love to his wife again, and she gave birth to a son and named him Seth, saying, "God has granted me another child in place of Abel since Cain killed him."

<u>26</u> Seth also had a son, and he named him Enosh. At that time people began to call on the name of the LORD.

Some variants of Traditional Witchcraft will also bear reference to this story regarding the famed 'mark of Cain' and will use this as a term that explains somebody having what's known as witch-blood. Witch blood meaning the person in question is a witch naturally, that the cunning fires of witchery course and pulsate through their veins. The mark seen as a physical mark (typically but not always) on the  brow, or a spiritual mark as a way to identify that person as a witch. A working that is sometimes performed in Traditional Witchcraft, is what we come to know as 'rousing the inner fire'. This working enflames and rouses the inner fire within the witch, empowering them and charging them ready for spell work but not only that, it helps release the potential the witch has of recognising the sacred Godhead within.

Rousing the Inner Fire

A practice many Traditional Witches may perform is an exercise which is known as: 'rousing the inner fire'. Remember earlier on? I mentioned the term: *the truth lies betwixt the horns*. This implies within each of us is that spark of divinity which is that inner witch fire which the Aulde one holds as the witch father and giver of magic. It also gives reference to the God Tubal Cain with whom his energy is lent in the following working given.

The following ritual is given so that the practitioner can not only have access to their inner fire but also to rouse it. To build it and to rise the fires up so that the witch becomes empowered for workings and you're able to cast effective magic. When performing this, you may feel a myriad of ways after, you may feel tingly all over, you may feel inspired, talkative, or even sexually aroused, it is genuinely not uncommon for these feelings to occur after performing this rite. This ritual is best completed in utter darkness, be that outside or indoors, keep all light (apart from the candle's flame) to a minimum.

Begin by facing the east, direction of the blacksmith and the rising sun, and sit cross-legged. Have in front of you a cauldron with a mix of suitable incense and a single-lit candle that's comfortable enough for you to hold with both hands. Take ten deep cleansing inward and outward breaths, and bring your awareness to your solar plexus, starting to envision a small fire alight. See in your mind's eye, a blacksmith bellows that are attached to your mouth that pushes into you air which will rise and ignite that inner fire. You have become the blacksmiths furnace.

As you breathe in, drop the candle down and see the flames lowering. Then as you breath out and into the bellows, lift the candle to your closed eye level envisioning and seeing and feeling your inner witch fire being kindled more intensely with each fan of the bellows. See this as you stir that inner fire, take your time doing this, and start to feel the physical change within yourself. How do you feel? Warm? Hot? Can you feel the energy around you? Take your time, and really feel and honour this moment. Now, after an amount of time continue to do this but there is a final drop down of the candle but this time, you're going to see your witch fire traveling out of your body all the way down, going deeper and deeper, into the earth, burrowing faster until your inner fire reaches a forge.

See your inner fire upon an anvil, and see a blacksmith with a mallet, this is Tubal Cain. Lord of black smithery and flame, see his leather apron, see his metal mallet and hear the clinking as the hammer strikes your inner fire upon the anvil, which triples it in size as it shoots back from the forge, back up from the deep earth and it hits your body, encompassing it and overtaking it completely by fire. Lift your candle up to your eye line, and take that moment to feel the energy all around yourself overtaking you and burning through all fear, all doubt, and literally overpowering you with sheer fire, flame, and witch power. Take your time to bathe in this power, bask in the light's sacred glow, and repeat the following:

"Fiery one, shining one, Ol Tubal of the seven tongues rouse the fires within me, Aulde Qayin first smith, first wizard, first of witch blood, by tongs and anvil by forge and flame, rouse the fire in your name!"

Repeat this last sentence to form a chant taking your time once again, feeling completely and utterly immersed within Qayins light and flame:

"By tongs and anvil, by forge and flame, rouse the fire in your name!"

This method is heavily inspired by Peter Paddon's grimoire for modern cunning folk, he is no longer with us and now in the spirit world, but I highly recommend this book. An interesting story connecting this rite, I was at one point in my practice having quite prominent doubts and it started affecting my actual workings the more I doubted the more I felt powerless, and many know this as 'imposter syndrome' which has become a popular talking point in recent years and for good reason as it can be nasty to a practitioner.

I remember distinctly feeling like I needed my power back, I needed to take back my confidence in the craft and take back my gnosis that as a witch and a practitioner I held the ability to weave power and affect the world around me.

I had an incredible urge to perform this ritual and at the time was using a glass candle for the ritual. I was doing the ritual and came to the part of shifting my inner fire to the blacksmith forge when during the moment I saw my witch fire upon the forge. I saw a mallet, but the mother of all mallets strike down upon my fire, and as my witch fire raised into my body every hair went up on the back of my neck and I genuinely for a split second felt like I was on fire, It felt so incredibly intense.

I just observed the moment even though at times it felt too intense to bear and felt it burning away everything. Every doubt, every single shred I had of no confidence was burning and on fire, and instead, I was being renewed like a snake shedding its skin. It felt incredible. After the ritual was complete, I left the glass candle on the floor as I went to make something to eat to ground myself. Just as I was about to walk down the corridor, I heard an almighty smash and ran back to the room. The glass candle had completely cracked in the middle. I was astonished and at that moment, knew that I shouldn't doubt myself or what I'm capable of magically and even not just magically just in general. It's safe to say, afterwards, the imposter syndrome went away.

Queen Of Elphame

Also known as the witch mother, the Queen of Elphame is the queen of the elf land, the land of the fae folk, and her rule is over it and its inhabitants. 'Elphame' or Elfame' is Pronounced 'Elf hame' or 'Elf-hammay' the term literally means elf home. The Queen is seen prevalent in the UK, but especially within north England and Scotland. What's interesting is North England and Scotland, in general, have some crossovers in terms of folklore such as the brownie or boggart. When it comes to the Queen of Elphame this too is prevalent. She is the queen of the faery folk, the wild woman in the woods who holds the knowledge of charms, and spells, and has dominion over the little people or good folk.

She is not only the queen of faery folk, but the queen of witches too and will happily take witches to the land of Elphame in order to teach them knowledge of witchery but it may come at a price. She is seen in the ballad of Thomas the rhymer, taking him to Elfame for a total of seven years.

Initially because of her beauty, he mistakes her for the virgin Mary but she corrects him:

"True Thomas he pull's aff his cap
And louted low down to his knee:
"All hail, thou mighty Queen o' Heaven!
For thy peer on earth, I never did see."
"O no, o no, Thomas," she said,
"That name does not belong to me;
I am but the queen of fair Elfland
That am hither come to visit thee."

In this tale and ballad, she wears a green dress of silk and wearing a mantle made of velvet. However, the poet Robert Cromek gave an intriguing description of her stating that she wears a long grey mantle and carries a wand, he also assumed her with another character known as the Gyre Carling:

"We will close our history of witchcraft with the only notice we could collect, of a celebrated personage called the Gyre Carline: who is reckoned with the mother of glamour, and near a-kin to Satan himself. She is believed to preside over the 'Hallowmass Rades' and mothers frequently frighten their children by threatening to give them to Mcnevin, or the Gyre CALINE. She is described as wearing a long gray mantle and carrying a wand, which, like the miraculous rod of Moses, could convert water into rocks and sea into solid land."

The queen of faery is also mentioned within different witch trials such as Andro man's familiar who swore to the Queen of Elphen. The queen also told Andro man that he would know all things and would help cure all sicknesses. Susan Swapper in 1607 claimed that when she first met the Queen of Elphame, she was told to kneel before the queen by a group of spirits. What's also interesting, is that a north country cunning man known as Webster was blessed with healing powers by the faery queen. Which he described how he entered a fair hall, where the queen was sat in great stature with many people around her, with the spirit that brought him to this place presenting him to the queen herself who told the cunning man that he was welcome. The Queen of Elphame has visited practitioners at different times in history in visions such as Fulham's cunning woman Alice West who claimed that the king and queen of faeries visited her in a vision.

Wherever we look she seems to be prominent and ever pervading keeping watch and influencing witches, cunning folk, and their practices.

Another name for her in Scotland is that of Nicnevin whose name means daughter of bones or daughter of saint, Nicnevin is equated to a Scottish Hecate in some ways. However, they are equally their own person and their own entity and after working with them both on separate occasions I can confirm they are very different entities to work with, but what hasn't helped this idea, is the fact that Sir Walter Scott had equated her to the Greek deity Hecate. Some may equate Nicnevin to a Goddess, however to me she is the queen of the good folk and so in doing so, I see her as more of a spirit rather than a Goddess (having said that, a God is just a large spirit). There has been speculation, however, that Nicnevin is a Pagan remnant from pre-Christian Britain.

This isn't a speculation that is new and can be seen in literature through the ages. For instance, in the book Demonologie written by James the 6th, he portrays the roman virgin Goddess Diana of the hunt as the ruler of the faery kingdom. He says the following:

"The fourth kind of spirits, which by the gentiles was called Diana and her wandering court, and amongst us is called fairy (as I told you) or our good neighbours".

King James in Daemonologie interestingly enough makes reference to the Queen of Elphame and the relationship between herself and the witches:

"Sundrie witches have gone to death with that confession, that they have been transported with the phairie to such a hill, which opening, they went in, and there saw a faire

queene, who being now lighter, gave them a stone that had sundrie virtues".

This is an occurrence that isn't new as mentioned, and especially when you read the section on the Devil. We can see that these Gods of the older religion were at times adapted into more infernal entities, that also bear an intrinsic connection to those of the fae or the good folk.

Perhaps The Queen of Elphame is herself an older Pagan Deity, but once again that is merely speculation at this point as we cannot be crystal clear of this. However, the evidence does point towards this which could be a possibility.

Nicnevin is said to be the queen of the Unseelie court, which is considered the darker aspects of the fae folk. Typically, the Unseelie court of faery folk as compared to the Seelie, are less favourable towards humans, not all the Unseelie are but this is typically the case.

The Queen of Elphame can visit people when she wants to, and as the queen of witches will see fit to visit different witches who call her name, or sometimes they don't need to. The feast days of Nicnevin are said to be on the 9th and the 11th of November, these nights she is said to take flight with various company in the sky, some folklore that is similar to the famous wild hunt.

Nicnevin can also be seen in poetry as far back as 1580 by Alexander Montgomerie, which interestingly makes use of her being known as the 'Elf Queen':

"Nicnevin with her nymphes, in number anew
With charms from caitness and chanrie of ross
Whos cunning consists of casting a ball of yarn
The king of faerie and his court, with the elf queen,
With many elvish incubi was riding that night."

Alongside this lore, November the 11th is not only the old calendar date for the Celtic festival of Samhain (come to be known now as Halloween) but also that of Martin mass. On this day, a cockerel or some animal would be slain, and the blood smeared over the door so that; if any blood was to be spilled for the year, it would be the blood spilled there and then and no one else's that resided in that household.

Such a ritual is synchronistic to that of Samhain being known as the blood harvest. A time where the cattle who wouldn't make it through the cold winters ahead, would be slaughtered and stored as meat for the long winters. The Queen of Elphame, like it or not has been integral (particularly within the witch trials in the early modern period) as an entity that coincides with the Witch Cult.

The Devil

Now we can come to a part of the book that can leave a bitter taste in the mouths of modern witches and Pagans. Quite often, (especially if you're a beginner in the craft) we hear the usual statement: REAL WITCHES DONT BELIEVE IN THE DEVIL! Well, I'm here to burst the bubble on that usual monotonous phrase, as Traditional Witches have been working with the Devil for a large period of time.

Yes, to some witches the Devil isn't a concept that's utilised within their craft and that's absolutely fine. However, we need only look into history, folklore, and folk magic, to evaluate and draw the conclusion that the Devil as an entity has always played a major figurehead in historical witchcraft.

Many will automatically think of the Christian ideology of Satan, but this is not so. To the Traditional Witch, the Devil is a lot more complexed than God's opposite. If we look towards older archaeological finds within Pagan society such as the Gundestrupp cauldron, we see that there has been a mysterious horned deity featured. We can see many horned Gods of history, and one only needs to look to find them; Pan god of nature to the Greeks, the image of Cernunnos bearing beautiful antlers to the Celts, Dionysis, god of vegetation was known as 'bull horned'.

Even if we look at other different religions aside from Paganism such as Hinduism, we see the horned God Pashupati known as Lord of all animals which interestingly at a glance of older images, we see a striking resemblance to

Cernunnos. That's not to indicate this Hindu God IS Cernunnos or vice versa, but it's interesting to see a similar comparison.

Horns play a prominent part within older Pagan cultures, as if crowning them not only with the powers of nature but with Godhead itself. Horned figures are a symbol of the perfect union betwixt mankind and beast. With the rise of Christianity, many believe that Christianity become forced and underwent aggressive conversations of people from the old religion to the new faith. However, this isn't necessarily true as it would have taken at least 200 years for a majority Christian conversion. Even Kings during this time period were dual faith between the old religion and the new. Such as King Rædwald who kept two altars in his temple, one Christian and one Pagan.

For the life of somebody at the time being dual faith, would involve going to church and worshipping Christ in a mass, and then going down to a well or a body of water and worshipping the old Gods.

However, once Christianity became the dominant religion in Britain and started to have its grip upon the laws of the land, the church saw those older representations of Pagan Gods bearing horns who weren't under the rule, who weren't controlled, who weren't restrained and represented man and beast formed in perfect unity, who weren't tame and who in fact were feral.

The image of this horned figure along with biblical references to the 'Anti-God' became the imagery for the Christian Satan we now have as the terrifying antichrist creature with horns and cloven feet. On top of this, this element of Christianity and Pagan leftover remnants developed into a large part of faery lore. This lore formed into folklore surrounding this figurehead, into what we now come to know as the Devil or the 'Aulde One' within Traditional Craft.

This enigmatic figurehead within the Old Craft is a mysterious character even to his followers, who acts as a bridge between the world of men and the world of spirits. He acts as a psychopomp and an opener of doors to the invisible world around us. He isn't defined by constraints or bound by sin, he is nature in its wildest and feral form.

We have the horned God within Wicca and the modern Pagan religions; however, the horned God is often considered the lighter side of nature. Whereas in Traditional Craft the Devil really is the wild, untamed, and free. He is the icy wind that blows through the crossroads at midnight, he is the fear we get when walking through a dark woodland in the pitch black of night that makes the hairs stand to attention at the back of our neck, he is a trickster and someone that will strike a deal with you but isn't afraid to find loopholes, emulating his association with the hidden folk and the faery faith as by nature they too are fond of loopholes within contracts.

The reason many fear him, the reason he strikes terror into the heart of men, is because he cannot be controlled. He cannot be tamed, he is unapologetically The Devil, King of faeries and Witch Lord incarnate. His association with witches can be seen in folklore and historical charms throughout the UK such as the Orkney witches charm documented in the 1880s by folklorist Walter Triall Dennison where a fledgling witch will lay within seven stones between the ebb and flow of the tide singing the well-known charm:

"O' Mester King o' a' that's ill,
Come fill me wi' the Warlock Skill,
An' I shall serve wi' all me will.
Trow tak me gin I sinno!
Trow tak me gin I winno!
Trow tak me whin I cinno!
Come tak me noo, an tak me a',
Tak lights an' liver, pluck an' ga,
Tak me, tak me, noo I say,
Fae de how o' da heed, tae da tip o' da tae.
Tak a' dats oot an' in o' me.
Tak hare an hide an a' tae thee.
Tak hert, an harns, flesh, bleud an banes,
Tak a' atween the 93rave stanes,
I' de name o' da muckle black Wallowa!"

The person must lie quietly for a little time after repeating the Incantation. Then opening his eyes, he should turn on his left side, arise, and fling the stones used in the conjuration into the sea. Each stone must be flung singly, and with the throwing of each a certain malediction was repeated.

In England, particularly East Anglia, a certain ritual which has its origins in the horseman's word, was performed known as 'the toad bone rite'. It involved the process of impaling a poor toad or frog on blackthorn until the toad passed away, to then input the body into an ant hill. Once the flesh from the bones had been picked off, the bones were then gathered by the witch who would throw them into a running river or stream. The bone that went against the running current, would sometimes scream going upstream and that would be the bone the witch had to grab in order to become a toad witch.

To be a toad witch would mean that the toad man or toad witch would have the ability to 'jade' those around them and animals which means to control. Not only that, but they were also said to hear the thoughts of animals and commune with them too. Make no mistake, but once the bone was collected, during this time there would be trials and tribulations. The witch themselves would have to in some accounts of folklore, venture to a cemetery or a stable and spend the night in it with them alongside the bone.

However, they would not be alone, The Devil himself was said to visit and to try and take the toads bone for his own. He would come to the witch during the night and it was the person's job to 'outwit or trick the Aulde One' into the witch owning the bone.

Across the globe, we see similar initiation rituals concerning the Aulde One in the guise of the Devil. In the book the silver bullet and other American witch stories compiled by Hubert J. Davis, we see an invocation invoking the Old One under the guise of the Devil which was said by Jonas Dotson as a pledge in order to become a witch which was said to be similar to be sworn by many witches at their initiation over the Atlantic:

"As I dip the water with the ram's horn,

Cast me, a cruel heart of thorn,
As I now to the Devil do my soul lease.
I also renounce Christ as my saviour
And promise the Devil me behaviour
Till my life on earth shall cease.
May my black and evil soul be
Of Christian love and grace free
As this place is of grease.
And when I become an evil crone
From outer skin to my inner bone
I'll never give Christians any peace."

He comes in many forms, a stranger by the crossroads, in some accounts of lore he is known as 'the man in black'. He can come as a goat, a black dog, even a black cat in various witch trials confessions and accounts. However, the most prominent form he is known for is that of half man and half beast, forming a merging of that perfect unity between man and nature emulating another aspect of the witch maxim *'all is one.'*

Speaking of maxims, a popular phrase that occurs within Traditional Witchcraft is the term known as: *'The truth lies betwixt the horns'* you may be thinking to yourself what does this mean?

To those of the Witch Cult, this term holds an element of Gnosticism here. For those not too familiar with Gnosticism, it is ultimately the belief that human beings contain within them a piece of Godhead. With this quote, it is entirely a similar definition. To the wise, this maxim means that between the horns of the Aulde One, lies that primordial witch fire. Within that fire, there lies that ability to cast magic as well as the ability to become as of the divine and connect with Godhead and so to the Traditional Witch, we have inside of us that same fire that the Old One holds between his horns. We not only have the ability to cast and conjure magic and create change in the world, but more importantly it is US that have direct access to Deity because an aspect of divinity is within us.

It is him who teaches us what to do with that power and how to use it in a way that not only makes a change in the world, but also empowers us. He ultimately is the God of the witches. Cecil Williamson also made comment on the truth lying betwixt the horns when mentioning a witches temple:

As in beygone times, the witches of today pay homage to the horned God. The symbolism of the horned God is the goat, stag, ram, or bull. For each is an ancient representation of the God of light, hence the lighted candle mounted between the horns. Light in the form of the living flame is a vital element in the mysticism of witchcraft. This temple was used for a number of years by a witchcraft group. Their rituals are a mixture of cabbalistic magic (as set forth in the key of Solomon.) and shamanic magic. Witches believe that their supernatural powers are given to them by 'the God of light'. Consequently, we find them devoting much time and labour to making gifts and sacrifices to this God's force in order to obtain continence in his favour. Such offerings were made in this temple.

If you want to find him, then you will need to venture to a crossroads in the dark of night and wait for him there. Ask him to make himself present and for him to come to you. You will feel a lot of fear, a lot of panic overtake you but eventually once you give yourself up and you allow it to completely overtake you, surrender to those more 'wilder' powers, then you'll experience and know him more than you ever could.

However, to those of the craft he can often come and be a part of your practice as and when he suits. After all, it is himself that gives out that divine spark to every person. The maker of his own rules, he can do whatever he likes.

He also goes by many different names to different witches and practitioners that may find names attached to him in different areas. For instance, in East Anglia, he is known as 'Aulde Harry' in Cornwall 'Bucca' in different areas he goes by different names due to lore and legend surrounding him. Some of these names are Aulde Hornie, Puck, Robin Goodfellow, Herne, The Man in Black, The De'il, Old Scratch etc.

Some of these names are attributed to him but originate from the faery folk such as Bucca or Robin Goodfellow. In fact, many of these entities are separate within themselves if we look into older stories and tales of them, different traditions of witchcraft can also interchangeably see these as representations of the Devil through different guises showing again the ties and dominion he has over the realm and world of the Good folk and spirits.

Old Fate

Fate is a term used by Traditional Witches to not only describe a preordained destiny set out for each living beings life and death, but it also describes the Gods. To the Traditional Witch it is not only them who makes the decisions but Fate itself as a concept and entity, ties into a much larger and primordial divinity.

A term you will see in some forms of Traditional Craft is 'Old Mother Fate' or 'Dame Fate' or 'The Pale Faced Goddess'. If the Queen of Elphame is considered the witch mother, then Dame Fate is the Grand Witch Mother of all.

When we often think of something being fated, we always envision something good and meaningful, but with Fate comes balance, and with every sweet comes the sour that's why we sometimes call her 'Cruel Mother Fate'.

She doesn't care about lasting relationships, she doesn't care about somebody's love for their family member, she has no attachments to those around her personally but yet all are attached through her web of Wyrd, connecting everyone and everything. She will absolutely have no qualms in bulldozing somebodies' life completely in order to get them to where they need to be so that Fate has its will and way with somebody.

To some practitioners, she isn't a deity that's called directly normally within their practice, as being Fate herself she is too far removed and governs spinning and weaving the threads of time and working her web of Wyrd. To some, they choose to work with her in their praxis, and feel she is constantly around everything, interwoven and interlinked building a personal relationship with all she touches. Just like everyones destiny and life, she has different meanings to different people.

Wyrd means the concept in Anglo Saxon culture roughly comparable to Fate or personal destiny. Just like the three Fates or the three Norns found within Greek and Norse mythology. It is her that weaves the webs of somebody's life, it is her that holds the cord of somebodies journey and lastly, it is her that with a scythe cuts the web extinguishing a living beings time on this earth sending them back to the invisible world. All things start with her, and all things end with her.

In the star-crossed serpent, Evan John Jones describes her as the one knowing our ultimate fate of the world. An entity that acts as the Alpha and Omega of all creation.
She is the weaver of Wyrd itself, the creator of Fate, and essentially is Fate itself.

Sometimes she is mentioned during the lighting of the balefire within the beginning of Traditional Witch rituals as the Grand Fiery Creatrix of all. A distaff can also be incorporated into rites of the witch cult, representing her as the 'grand weaver'. Dame Fate is an entity that is often felt to be too far removed to establish a close personal relationship with, but with whom we all have a close personal relationship with as she is intricate to the existence of everything and every thread of Fate itself. She is infinity, she was there at the very beginning, and she will be there at the very end.

She is the one who pulls the cord, who holds the cord, and who cuts the cord. She is the *Mater Mundi,* the *textor,* and the *susceptor animarum* all at the same time. The Mother of the world, the weaver of cords, and the taker of souls. The

Alpha and Omega, she is everything and nothing. As fiery Creatrix, she is life, death and rebirth and so much more.

The Liminal World: Spirit Work Within the Ways Of The Witch

"I'd say to a person who wanted to know what the spirit of witchcraft was, that they'll learn more by going out to the downs at midnight and listening to the wind in the trees and looking at the full moon. They'll learn more of the spirit of witchcraft, the real spirit of witchcraft that way than they will be by reading any amount of books."
 -Doreen Valiente Power of the witch documentary 1979

A prominent part of the practice of witchcraft is working with what's known as the 'Genus Loci' also known as the Spirit of the land. Within the Witch Cult, the idea of animism or animistic practice is heavily integrated and plays a key part which can be seen throughout history, charms, and lore. The oxford definition of animism is: *'the belief that plants, objects, and natural things such as the weather have a living soul.'*

That definition is no different regarding the land we're working with, the Genus Loci is the spirit of the place in which you're working in magically. Quite often, with various practitioners there will be a natural space that a witch will have regular practice with, as well as a deep spiritual bond with the land and spirits having worked there regularly.

Once rapport and a decent relationship are built with the spirits of the land, you will honestly never look back in your practice. It is a beautiful experience to look up at the trees during a ritual, seeing the balefire's reflection on the leaves and branches, and feel completely a part and connected to the land you're standing on. The spirits of the land will help, guide, and assist you in your magic as well as align you with the place you're working with. Sometimes they can do this in ways that help your practice when you're unaware of what they're doing at the time. For example, a long while back when I first started practicing Traditional Witchcraft, I had chucked myself into practicing but with not a lot of research or knowledge under my belt about different aspects of the tradition, this I don't regret as it was this way I learnt best.

When I used to lay a compass round, I would light a candle after the witch ring was cast and state: *"I light this candle for the spirits of the land."* At the time I had absolutely no idea of the Genus Loci within Traditional Witchcraft practices or even the role it played, it was something that came completely and utterly natural to me. Being new to the nameless arte in general, I had doubts as to whether I was even on the right track or practicing properly. However, upon realising just how integral working with the spirits of the land was to Traditional Craft, I then knew I was being guided well by the Genus Loci.

Just exactly like people, each Genus Loci will differ in personality, openness, and friendliness. The lands are different and will have different attitudes toward humans in general. Some will enjoy human company and even gift them items whilst some will actively hate human company, and this may be for a myriad of reasons. Two examples of this which I've personally experienced, is that a while back (about seven years ago) I was staying with a coven down south around the midlands area in a beautiful ancient forest for Beltaine weekend.

Here I had the absolute honour of participating in the rituals and celebrations of Beltaine which were incredibly deep, purposeful, and beautiful. After the rituals were complete, we would then all continue the celebrations into the evening, this would quite often involve a bottle of alcohol that could strip walls and a cheeky bit of what the older generation called 'the Devil's lettuce. In other words, after drinking half a brewery and smoking half of Amsterdam, we ended up looking like absolute delights.

Each evening, I would fall into my tent and have the same stick digging into my back. It was a beautiful piece of hazel, twisted by honeysuckle vines creating a gorgeous serpentine curve within it. However, being mangled I would shout out: *"This f***ing stick!"* launching it out of the tent from which everybody there would be in tears of laughter. Well, this wasn't the end of colourful language I called it as it kept reappearing in my tent over and over again. At one point I launched this stick out of the tent calling out *"Ohhh you dirty bitch"* as it hit one of the coven summoners who again was in absolute stitches joking about how I was being stalked by a stick.

The Sunday evening, yet the twiggy little stalker was there again chilling in my tent. As I was about to throw it out and proclaim: *"dear Christ this stick"* my good friend Ange looked at me and said: *"No bab. That's meant for you, it keeps appearing, so it wants to go home with you. You've given the forest spirits offerings all weekend, it's a gift from the Gods of the woods."* She was bang on the money with that statement. That hazel stick is now my wand, we started on hilariously messy terms, but that same wand gifted to me by the spirits has helped create some beautiful and potent magic.

The second story is a bit more sinister, but an example of how not all land spirits want to be friends with you or enjoy human interaction or company. Ten years back, I went on a drive with an ex-boyfriend to the Yorkshire moors. For those of you that don't know, the moors have a dark history and have been witness to some awful crimes including the abduction, rape, and murder of innocent children by evil murderers Richard Brady and Myra Hindley.

For some reason, we decided to drive in the night and ended up on the top of the moors. As we were sitting in the car the person driving turned the lights off from the inside of the car. It was as if the darkness from outside seeped into the vehicle creating this cold, void, blackness that felt so uneasy.

It was awful, the last cherry on the cake was when we were outside, and my ex and another person started running as they felt they were being chased. We all frantically ran into the car screaming and frantic to start the vehicle. Once the car was started, we floored it and sped away like maniacs because of how frightened we were. I can't describe it fully, but it was terrifying. Literally like the land wanted us out of there as soon as possible and I would not for a million pounds work spiritually in that place personally. That's me personally, as the Yorkshire moors are huge. However, the overall feeling I got was that the land DID NOT want company at all.

Rituals To Honour The Land Spirits

With these two stories in mind, and going back to the original quote by Doreen Valiente, you really will come to learn more about the Genus Loci by actually going to the land and experiencing the spirits themselves. There's a really simple way to start establishing a bond with the spirits of the land.

This can be done by just lighting a candle as mentioned in the beginning after you lay your compass round and stating: *"I light this fire for the spirits of the land."* But mostly, the best way to start is to do something to benefit the land itself. Such as going around with a couple of black bags and picking up rubbish. Clear up the place, as my good friend Jonathan says: *"what's the point of honouring the land if you're not going to do something that HONOURS and BENEFITS the land."* His completely right! Start small by going and cleaning up the place and make a statement of intention before you do this:

"I'm doing this to honour the spirits of the land and the animals and lifeforms that reside within it. Honour to thee"

The next step is for one to give regular offerings to the land, and this is simple. Firstly, please make sure you're somewhere you cannot be disturbed by any other human activity. There's nothing worse than having a spiritual moment, and then Dave's dog comes obnoxiously strolling through and treats himself to a cheeky offering right bang in the middle of your ritual, or a cyclist thinking he's doing the tour de France going right through your rite. I'm not even kidding, all these situations have happened to me and they're infuriatingly frustrating and just take you out of the moment.

So please for the love of the Gods, try to find a place that is private and away from nosey parkers. Give offerings that will benefit the land youre working in once again. Seeds are a great offering especially wildflower seed mixes you can buy as they help the land by bringing more flowers to the area whereby giving the bees more flowers to pollinate. Offer bread, eggs, milk, and meats, are all things that can be consumed by the wildlife on the land. Try to avoid things like high sugary sweets or chocolate that are poison to some animals. A good symbol to make an offering on is the forest spirit sigil, given by Sarah Ann Lawless in her previous blog witch of forest grove. This can be drawn on the floor using bonemeal or flour.

Stand in front of the sigil and look around your surroundings. Look at the trees, the plants, the ground below your feet, is there water? Take some time to look the land around you, hear the sounds of the birds chirping merrily, listen to the wind and rustling of the trees, and take it all in. Take some time to just be. Be in the moment and appreciate what's going on around you and the other lifeforms in this beautiful and sacred place. Then take ten deep and calming breaths. Inhaling deeply through the nose and exhaling calmly through the mouth, once this is done state the following:

"Hail to thee Genus Loci Spirit of place and spirits of the land I came today and bring offerings and honour to your name, most beautiful and powerful spirit of place. Hear my call and accept this sacrifice I give unto you. So be it"

Lay the offerings in the middle of the sigil crossroads, and then close your eyes in meditation for a few moments. Just focusing on the land and the animals you've seen, and encountered today in this place. After the rite, look for any omens or signs from the land if there aren't any don't worry, they will come eventually. You should 'know' if the land has accepted these offerings, it's something you will sense within yourself. Afterwards, walk away without looking back, leave these offerings for the animals around you and the spirits of the land.

The very first time I performed this ritual was with a good friend of mine and craft partner Jonathan Phoenix-Archer. After we had performed this rite in a place free of prying eyes, we noticed that we were surrounded by trees that formed a perfect circle. So with that, we instinctively started to clear out some space removing debris to form this circle. We just had this feeling that the space was meant for us as a regular working site. It was summer at the time, and such beautiful weather so the next day we came back with tools and henged a massive circle, topping it up with each visit and giving regular offerings.

Then, overtime we started to put stones in the four directions of the circle's edge and even created a miniature altar complete with outdoor hood lamps one of blackthorn and one of white thorn. The space was a truly beautiful place that held fond and magical memories for us both and others. Not only this, but it also even emitted some strange phenomenon. I distinctly remember making that journey towards the woods, during winter and having this feeling that the space was like a warm home as I was so cold. I always used to think: *"Once we're in the space we'll be warmed up"* and we were.

Once stepping into the space, it had its heat and acted like a shield against the elements. That was only the start of it, as a myriad of strange occurrences would happen and leave me and Jonathan truly baffled. Even by writing this, I don't think I'm doing the whole experience and space justice.

The amount of beautiful, soulful, and truly influential moments we had in that special place was insane and its genuinely a place with such intense spiritual moments that for the rest of my life I will always remember, and I thank Jonathan for those moments as well as the woods it was based in. Now, let me make myself clear regarding the given ritual.

I'm not saying that by performing the ritual supplied earlier, you will automatically be gifted with a space that will bring you all these experiences. That was not our intention at all, and I don't feel that this ritual is designed for that. I just think the spirits at the time realised we would be feeding them regularly and saw our intentions and we got lucky. Very lucky indeed. However, I know for a fact this simple ritual as simple as it was, formed a connection with the spirits of the land and would eventually be the predecessor for a deeply spiritual bond and an unforgettable relationship with that space.

Listen to the Land

Obviously from what I've written so far concerning the spirits of the land and forming an avid working relationship with them, it's SO important to listen to the signs and what happens when out in the land. This is the way spirits can communicate to you through omens also known as synchronicities. Once you follow that route and start listening to those omens, you'll find that you're not only connecting with the spirits but it changes your mindset and your entire frame of mind. You learn to trust not only the spirits you're working with, but yourself and your instincts too. I want to tell you another story that happened to myself and a friend Suzanne one evening down at Pennington flash in Leigh where we would occasionally drive to in the evenings to perform rituals and workings there.

It was on the way there I grabbed some cream at the local supermarket, as it is a traditional offering. I knew that it was needed for that evening and had this overwhelming urge to get it and bring it as an offering to ritual. As well as cream, we bought flowers to lay down onto the land and give to the lake as an offering. The moment we pulled up in the car, it was pitch black but illuminated by the lights was a juvenile and feral kitten who had ran out of a nearby bush just as the lights shone onto the bushes, from which both of us being big animal lovers both exclaimed simultaneously a loud AWWWWW!

Once we pulled up and got out of the car, we were opening the boot for supplies and the firewood we had bought. By our feet, we heard a little meow with the kitten going around our legs affectionately. We were so happy and gave him a stroke and a little cuddle, and that sealed the deal. Our little friend had decided to come with us the whole way to our working site and was literally walking in front of us. With that, we decided to follow him as we felt we were being 'lead' in a way and eventually got to a site by the lake which was completely concealed from any human activity.

We set up our working tools and began to perform our ritual and working. The whole time this beautiful little feline was there, walking around in circles, meowing, and then coming for cuddles during our workings. So, there we were, sat by the side of a lake lit up by the brightest full moon you've ever seen, complete with a big cauldron holding within it a gorgeous blazing fire, and a beautiful cat sat by us as we were chanting. I have to be honest, it was perhaps one of the most witchy moments of my life! Suzanne agreed with the same thing.

It's funny because the whole time we couldn't help but think our little pal had guided us into this spot and was there for a reason. Then when about to lay down the offerings it dawned on us that this little guy was a physical representation of the spirits of the land. It was him who had guided us, it was him who was there with us and it was him who was about to take some of the cream and take the offering! This beautiful little animal was the physical embodiment of the land spirits of Pennington Flash.

It was such a beautiful moment that words cannot explain, and the thought dawned on me that perhaps I should take the little fellow home. He had no collar on and despite being friendly gave us the impression he was feral. When it was time to head back home, he walked us out of this secluded spot once again towards the bushes where he had first run out of, and then just ran off completely disappearing from us, and I knew that I wasn't meant to take him home.

I never saw my little pal again, but I am fully convinced he was an embodiment of the spirits of the land that night. It was them that guided us to a safe secure working site, it was them that added to our ritual, and it was them that saw we got back to the car safe.

This was perhaps one of the many magical moments in my life where I've felt the influence of spirits highly, and not every time and moment will be like the latter. These things can happen if you just open your mind and allow yourself to be guided by the spirits, be respectful, show them reverence and respect as you're on their patch.

You are the one that is on their home and just like entering any home, say hello! Be respectful to them, arrange days where you go and collect litter from that specific place, and keep giving regular offerings. These things build rapport with the spirits of the land and yourself and form an avid relationship.

Not only that, but it's also nice to tidy up a place from the ravages of human activity and to just be respectful to the animals around. I hope this wee story indicates how listening to the spirits and allowing yourself to follow their guidance really can result in beautiful and substantial experiences. Because I know I will never forget that moment, and it will stay with me for the rest of my life as it was so profound, and genuinely was touching.

The Mighty Dead and Tapping the Bone

The Mighty Dead are a key part of the praxis for most Traditional Witches. A lot of Pagan forms of witchcraft will work with their ancestors during the time of Samhain. However, to the Traditional Witch the ancestral dead are spirits that are worked with the whole year round. When we think of The Mighty Dead, we're thinking of course of our initial ancestors we would have known in our lifetimes.

Those ancestors who have had an impact upon our lives, who have made us into the people we are today, whose lessons and love we carry into this life and passing it on to others making their love and their compassion infinite.

When venerating The Mighty Dead, we are thinking of our nans, our great grandparents, and family members that may have sadly passed earlier than expected whom we affected upon. Ancestral worship and veneration are one of the easiest ways of accessing spirit work because your ancestors are a given, they have made you into whom you are, and even those ancestors who you may not have known, but whose stories may inspire, shock, or intrigue you. All those ancestors who had their tears and the laughter, their struggles, their hardship, and their joyousness, all contributed to you as a person coming into existence.

Ancestral worship is such a special thing because by venerating and empowering our ancestors, were not only venerating them and elevating the ancestral spirits but because the link between themselves and you are so connected you're also elevating and venerating yourself.

Those who are perhaps adopted may struggle with this concept, or who may not have been entirely close to their ancestors may not feel a connection to this. I understand how such a practice from that perspective may seem daunting perhaps or even confounding as of where to start. Our friends quite often are the family or 'tribe' we choose for ourselves, they are people that we chose to love and have connections to.

For myself, I count my friends that have sadly passed away early as ancestors. They may not be connected by blood, but they are connected by love. There's something incredibly beautiful about the relationships we form as humans, as well as the influences they hold over us in our lives. If you think this only applies to humans also, then you may be mistaken as animals are no different. They are our little friends we've again chosen to have in our lives where bonds have been created between ourselves and them. They become our own family in our lives, and this is something that again adds to the spiritual clan we come to know as The Mighty Dead.

To those of the craft, by honouring those ancestors we are also connecting to the spiritual thread of the old Pagan religions. Now don't get me wrong, we don't physically commit sacrifices of humans or animals to the Old Gods, such has been documented throughout history.

Times have moved on, but we do give offerings of straw figures as a sacrifice, particularly on the festival of Lammas. The sacred dead and their connection to the land are prominent within the beliefs of the witch and merge quite often with the ancient fairy faith, known also as the 'hidden folk' or the 'good folk' there are various mentions, particularly regarding faery lore and the dead.

Burial mounds being an ancient resting place of The Mighty Dead were also entrances to the Otherworld of the fairy folk. An example is the fairy toot in north somerset which is said to be the place where many a faery and goblin have been seen. The burial mound in north Yorkshire is known as the pudding pie hill, is said that if you run around the burial mound nine times and stick a knife in the top of it, you can hear the faeries. The burial Cysts in Shetland are said to be haunted and that 'peerie' (tiny) hill men can be encountered. These burial mounds are often known within folklore as 'faery mounds' the belief that these ancient resting places of The Mighty Dead are also the home of the little people.

The witch sees no coincidence between the burial mounds and the good folk, and see's this as something in folklore suggesting the ancient dead and the faery realm are inexplicably linked together. In the trials of Alison Pearson in 1588, it was said that when she would venture down to Elphame and having met the 'good neighbours' would see many dead friends and relatives that were said to heal her by God's will.

Beliefs regarding the dead or the afterlife in Traditional Craft belief systems will differ, for instance in the Clan of Tubal Cain and some other working groups, there is the belief in reincarnation. Some Traditional Witches (like myself) see the ancient dead as those of the 'hollow hills' in other words; the ancient dead become part of the land and merge with them causing a deep spiritual transformation and metamorphosis, becoming more than just the human dead they become that of the fae over time. Some may personally experience this regarding the dead and the faery folk. Particularly among those who are clairvoyant but those spirits that have passed away for a long amount of time always seem very different to those who in contrast have died recently.

For instance, there is a huge difference between a spirit who passed away in the 1950s, compared to somebody who died in the 1600s. This isn't just mentioning the cultural and historical predicaments, but the latter not only have a more ancient feel to them. They also feel so far gone that they've become and metamorphosised into something different and almost don't feel as human as those who have passed away recently.

I'm not suggesting all those who passed away in the 1600s are now faery folk, but put this into context and see that the dead older than the 1600s as in the truly ancient dead that go back to neolithic times have at this point undergone a spiritual metamorphosis and deep transformation and become 'of the good folk'.

To connect to the sacred dead, the witch will perform what's known as tapping the bone, a ritual in which two bones are tapped together creating and forming a rhythmic, shamanic, sound to tap into and connect with the dead. The ritual below gives instructions for this, but it is a way in which we connect with our ancestors.

Tapping the Bone

To begin, have yourself a bone long enough to bang upon a skull of an animal such as a goat's skull, a deer's skull, etc. If you haven't got any of these that's ok, for the witch wanting to travel to the woods compactly, two bones large enough to bang together will suffice and they can be ANY bones. Don't worry, they can even be chicken bones as long as they have been prepared in a sufficient way, and not straight out of a KFC bargain bucket. To prepare the bones, make sure all the flesh is stripped away from them and boil them up until everything else apart from the bone falls away.

Once boiled, leave the bones out in the sun to naturally bleach and dry. Once dried, rubbing them very lightly in an oil such as ylang ylang or lily will help fuel the otherworldly influence upon them, and leave them once more to dry again in the sun. Do not use salt for these bones at all, the dead aren't a fan of salt and it's something that is found in many other different spiritistic traditions too such as Haitian Vodou, where they believe the ancestors can't eat anything with salt. Salt is often mentioned too within British folklore to deter away spirits.

Venture to a graveyard, and take some sprigs of the yew plant and immerse in within a bottle of water for use in the ritual. The sacred yew is a tree commonly associated with the powers of the dead and is heavily attributed to the dead, so be certain to leave an offering down for the spirits in the cemetery and for the yew you're taking. On a more practical note, please be careful and make sure to wash your hands after handling, as yew is poisonous.

Make some incense up of Myrrh as a base, mugwort which is said to call up the dead by burning it, some grated and dried out apple considered the legendary 'food of the dead', lavender to bring peace to the dead, 4 drops to represent the crossroads of Lilly of the valley fragrance oil or ylang ylang, both fragrances associated heavily with the dead. On top of this, add a small pinch of graveyard dirt (preferably taken from an ancestors grave). Alongside this, venture to a garden centre store and pick up some bonemeal, which is used as a plant fertiliser as the ground up bones and flesh of animals and is great for employing those otherworldly influences, especially that of The Mighty Dead.

With this bonemeal, you're to draw a particular sigil that I have created and worked with for years when calling and working with The Mighty Dead. Admittedly I wasn't going to employ this sigil within my books, but it feels like the sigil needs to be out there and given to people. To begin with, the bonemeal, draw the following sigil, in the middle of the working ground:

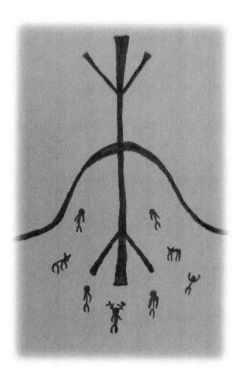

Take the water and pour it around the compass edge repeating the following:

"Be thoust a river of souls, a liminal place betwixt worlds, by the River Styx, by the powers of the west and the setting sun, by the aulde Yew, and by The Mighty Dead, I conjure thee o river of souls a meeting point between the quick and the dead. Be thou a bridge to welcome the ancestors in"

From this point, take the time to envision and see around you an otherworldly river that encompasses you. See it glowing bright, seeing the ancestral dead moving around within this river. Take the time to solemnly welcome them, by bowing your head down and keeping them all in memory. All those recent ancestors you remember, and the time spent and memories you once shared, take the time to send them your love and respect.

Once you've taken a moment to honour the ancestors, light some of the incense by the sigil that you have crafted and laid upon the floor. Saying a few words of offering towards your ancestors as you light the incense in their names:

"I light this incense in the name of my ancestors, I give it as an offering to them may its sweet fragrances sweeten our relationship we have."

Now, take your bones and hit them three times slower. Tap, tap, tap. Pause and repeat this bang, bang, bang. Keep the focus on your ancestors here, your ancestral lineage. Think of the ancestors whom you remember and even those mentioned by relatives with whom you are unaware. Repeat the banging of the bones tap, tap, tap.

Start to create a regular rhythm here with this. Start slow and eventually you're going to speed up fast. Now keep mindful of the ancestors lost in the seas of time but never forgotten. The ancestors that were alive the time of the ancients who built the burial mounds, the very ancient dead tap, tap, tap. Keep this repeating the whole time meditating on the different aspects of your ancestors and start to chant the following:

"I call on the ancestors of blood and bone, hear my call the lost and known"

See the ancestors, see all of their faces, see them coming from the river of souls you've created circling all around you. See all of their faces within yours, as you realise and take the time to know and keep mindful that without the ancestors you wouldn't be here. They are fundamental and integral to your being on this earth, all their struggles, all their journeys made, all their tears, all their laughter has to lead up to you at this moment.

You are them and they are you. Keep mindful of that. Now, take this moment to offer up to the ancestors some offerings of food to elevate your ancestors and to build them up in power. Perhaps they had a favourite food? Did a certain aunt like snuff? Did your beloved nan love bread and butter pudding? What about a cup of tea? These are all things to offer out to the ancestors, offer these foods on the sigil, thank your ancestors for their presence during your ritual, take the items you need, leave the food in the sigil. When you're ready to head home, walk away and don't look back.

The Familiar Spirit

Puckerill, ally, spirit companion, these are all names for what is essentially known within the Old Craft as the familiar spirit. Many will associate the familiar with a physical animal and this can sometimes be the case. Such as the witch of Kings Cross Rosaleen Norton, who had a rat named Pied Percy which she would call her familiar. Sybil Leek had a Jackdaw who would accompany her, these physical pets are very much familiars in their ways. However, much of the time a familiar is an actual spirit and this is something that is seen throughout history, lore, and praxis. But what is a familiar spirit? What role does it play when it comes to the witch and their craft?

To put it simplistically, a familiar spirit is a spirit that has an avid relationship and deep companionship with the witch. A friendship and 'familiar' bond that deeply connects the witch to that spirit which in tune bridges the earthly and invisible world together. That's one of the key things that a familiar spirit does, they bridge the two worlds together helping the witch keep one foot in this world and one foot in another. And so by working with the familiar spirit, they help the witch become liminal. The familiar spirit also becomes a messenger for the witch bringing them knowledge of the Otherworld along with its charms, spells, and invocations.

A familiar spirit will guide the witch within their craft and practice, inspiring them with spells, charms, and even giving instructions on how to perform the working. This is something that is quite often personal for me within my practice. When I need to perform a working and I've told other witches, through their good intentions they've suggested different methods of working magic that may help. However, by that point normally the familiar spirit has told me what to do and how to perform the working so that it will work effectively.

Normally this information can come through in a dream state or just an image along with words being put into my head repeatedly. It can take different forms for different people, but once you build up that trust and closeness with your Puckerill you just 'know' when it is them. This can be described very much the same way that you know when a good friend is behind you and puts their hands over your eyes as a way for you to guess. Providing you treat them well, and you don't abuse them (much in the way of any friendship) a familiar spirit will always have your back and have your best interests at heart. With this in mind, the familiar spirit acts also as a guide and if we look towards history, we can see it in the museum of witchcraft which shows a dried frog who was said to be a spirit guide and helper named 'Ben' by witch Sarah Noakes of Crewkerne in 1922.

Another aspect the familiar will cover is protecting and warding you away from what I like to call 'nasties'. Unfortunately, the fact is that not all spirits will have your best interests at heart. There will be some spirits that will want to harm you with false intentions. Other practitioners also may want to send you harmful or baneful magic and the familiar spirit will guard you or alert you against this in different ways for you to understand. Overall, the familiar ally will protect and guard you, warding away evil and malicious entities and spells that wish to do you harm.

You Scratch My Back; I'll Scratch Yours

Spirits work well with pacts or promises made and carried out. An example of this could be:. *'If you do this for me, il get you the eucharist as an offering'* or if you're aware that a familiar is more than partial to a certain type of food: *'Ok Finius, if you perform this task, then il get you some rich, creamy, delicious and thick full-fat cream that I know you like'.* Always making sure you deliver and carry out on those promises. The best relationship with any spirit isn't bribing or exploiting, it's carrying out promises and most of all establishing trust between yourselves.

Working with familiar spirits is an ancient practice and is even mentioned in the bible, but more notoriously we see a lot more evident practices from the early modern period onwards. In the case of accused Dagenham witch Joan Prentice in 1589, it was said she had a ferret who when first meeting climbed onto her lap and said: *"fear me not, my coming unto thee is to do thee no hurt... if thou wilt have me do anything for thee, I am and will be always ready at thy commandment."*

Interestingly and conveniently, because a lot of offerings given to familiar spirits back in the early modern period were of extreme value compared to the present day, these offerings are a lot more readily accessible to us now than compared in the early modern period. For instance, offerings such as bread, meat, beer, butter, milk, cream, and cheese were highly sort offerings that were suitable for the familiar spirit. Emma Wilby in her incredible book *Cunning folk and familiar spirits: shamanistic visionary traditions in early modern British witchcraft and magic*, writes how Bread was a popular offering and has been documented within different periods and places such as Elizabeth Francis who in 1566 claimed that her familiar 'Sathan' was given an offering of bread and milk that had been instructed by her grandmother. On the date of 1645, Mother Moone was said to feed her twelve imps with bread and beer.

As mentioned, the fact that historically and particularly through cases of witch trials bread plays an integral part in this shows us that bread in general is (depending on the familiar's request of course) a sufficient and suitable offering to give to the spirits.

A further idea is that in my experience spirits LOVE handmade things by humans. They appreciate the time being taken and the efforts by people's hands of things being made and this doesn't just stop at handmade gifts for the spirit world, this also carries into food.

A while back a familiar I was once equated with, would love nothing more than when I baked my bread that she was the first one to have the 'first bake'. This meant I would create an entirely separate (but mostly smaller) bit of bread for her in the shape of a roll and that is something that meant the absolute world to her. We have since then parted separate ways amicably, but the overall ending of the relationship was in both our best interests. Nevertheless, making and creating something from scratch, such as bread even if it is from a packeted bread mix DOESN'T MATTER. It's the love and input that you put into it that counts and spirits appreciate that.

Another aspect of offerings to familiar spirits is that of blood. It is my own opinion that by doing this, the witch themselves becomes inexplicably linked with the familiar spirit and they become one, forming an intimate bond and companionship. Such an act of giving blood to a familiar spirit should be performed once an avid relationship is established, and you're sure that familiar spirit's intentions are pure is a sure-fire way to connect you both deeper to each other. Such examples of giving blood can be seen in the ways of history once more where we see in the case of Ellen Shepeard 1646, who claimed that four familiars in the shape of grey rats had established that if they were to have blood from her that they would grant her 'all happiness'. We see also the belief of the Traditional Witch's mark being a mole or blemish on the body, which was used as a teat by familiar spirits to access the witch's blood to feed on.

I want to add a disclaimer, I have over the years had people contact me telling me they prick their moles and feed familiar spirits. PLEASE DO NOT prick or cut your moles it is extremely dangerous to do so and can cause cancer. Do not do it, it is quite frankly stupid. If you're wanting to draw blood from yourself in a healthy manner to feed spirits, then take advantage of what we have access to. Medical Lancets are a great way to draw blood healthily and will ensure you won't go putting yourself at risk. Pricking the finger (especially the left), and offering blood that way is a much more efficient and less harmful way if you're wanting to give blood as an offering.

Transformation and Form

Familiars take very different forms and can approach each practitioner in different ways especially concerning what is written in various accounts and lore. One could write an entire book primarily just on the familiar spirit and various aspects of practice encompassing them. For some, they've appeared as mice, rats, moles, cats, hares, imps, small faery women, handsome men, and even as childlike creatures that suck blood! The ranges of anthropomorphic and bestial forms taken do vary, and it is possible for a familiar spirit to also change its form. This is seen in different accounts, such as in 1646 Jane Wallis had said her two familiar spirits Grizzell and Greedigut came in several shapes most commonly as hounds with bristles on their backs.

I can also attest from the experiences I've had that I've had a similar experience when working with a familiar spirit and they've changed their form to suit the task given to them at hand. Once I asked a familiar spirit to be discreet about a working, and so they took the form of a mole so that they were able to 'burrow under the ground and be present without being spotted'.

Believe it or not, familiars in the form of angels were also popular with witches and cunning folk but rarely mentioned as much due to the infernal accusations and associations the courts were trying to attach to the accused. In the case of Andro man, he claimed that he possessed a familiar who was in the likeness of a fair angel clad in white clothes who swore his allegiance to the Queen of Elphame. In the grimoire of Arthur gauntlet, a seventeenth-century London cunning man's book of charms, conjurations, and prayers edited by David Rankine, holds various methods to conjure angelic beings. One such method worked within the book, is that of conjuring an angel into a glass of water, which after having completed such a ritual I can attest to its accuracy!

Another character mentioned within Gemma Gary's book Silent as the trees, were known as Old Marian Voaden. Who mentioned angelic beings pervading over her as she slept in her house that was at the time falling apart: *"my dear there be two angels every night sits on the rungs of the ladder and watches there, that nobody comes near me, and they be ready to hold up the timbers that they don't fall on me".*

She would recite the well-known traditional charm over burns or scalds over the affected area, perhaps she was incorporating the angels that watched over her. This again is speculation but looking over the charm one does wonder:

> *"There were three angels who came from the north,*
> *one bringing fire, the other brought frost,*
> *the other he was the holy ghost.*
> *In frost! Out fire! In the name etc."*

The familiar spirit isn't always worked with by Traditional Witches, but it is a thing that has very large historical ties to the practice and art of witchcraft in general and can be seen in so much lore, so many witch trials, and even ballads themselves.

The familiar spirit in my own opinion, or spirits you have a working familiar relationship with, is completely and utterly integral to witchcraft. Whether those familiars be an ancestral shade or ancestors, in general, you've become accustomed to, whether that be what's known as a faery counterpart, perhaps a beloved pet who passed away and was always 'there' when you cast magic, an imp or demon, an angelic being, Genus Loci of place and land you work in, the list will vary. Even so much as a plant you work with regularly such as vervain for instance; if you're always working with vervain in your practice and you speak to it each time you perform a working with, you will essentially begin to form a bond or relationship with that spirit.

In essence this is spirit work, and it is in my experience that as mentioned, spirit work to traditional-based witchcraft is integral. If you already do these things and you invite those spirits into your work then in my experience you've already got a spirit with which a strong foundation of familiarity is based, and you're able to build on that bringing them into your work more and eventually acquiring them as a familiar spirit.

Because the familiar spirit is so integral to my work, I will always include in a majority of my books ways in which somebody can acquire a familiar spirit. There will be two types of rites herein involving acquiring these familiar spirits that I am going to mention. One is what's known as the Alraun or Mandrake and another which is known as *'the faery counterpart'*. In true faery nature, let's go topsy turvy with this and delve deeper into the latter. When working with the little people or fae folk, it is quite evident that they have their own world and in truth their own ways.

Practitioners working with the good folk is something that's noted a lot through history and the fae folk and familiar spirits at times go hand in hand such as earlier mentioned with Andro Man's familiar spirit who swore to the Queen of Elphame or 'elf home'. Arthur gauntlet also mentioned earlier, within his grimoire had operations that would call the faery folk such as calling and invoking the seven faery sisters. Incidentally, I could go more and more into the faery folk but throughout this book, there is a myriad of different lore concerning the little people as their realms and worlds do intercept with the ways and lore of the witch.

A faery counterpart will keep you safe, they will protect you and they will bridge a gap in which you stand between the world of mortals and the faery folk. Acquiring such a familiar in truth is relatively easy, but you have to ensure that it's something you're wanting to do. They are only really suitable if the person is wanting to venture and work more within the realms of the fae and have those associations with them, just be warned the fae have their own ethics and morals. The faery folk and their world are something I go more into depth with in my first book Barbarous Words. Whilst we're on the subject of this and familiar allies, I'd like to add that I also include within Barbarous Words, a ritual of employing an animal's skull and conjuring a familiar spirit.

Interacting with The Familiar

Many will ask, how do I go about seeing the spirits and interacting with them? Which is an incredibly valid question when concerning spirit work. Cecil Williamson made mention that the witch was never be lonely, for she has her familiar spirit by her side. He also goes onto add that unlike most people, witches are endowed with a 'third eye' which once opened the world becomes an entirely different place. *'People have eyes but see not, ears and not hear not.'* The third eye is an interesting concept as it stems from the Chakras, the seven energy points in the body originating from India and is a truly ancient concept. What's interesting, is Cecil makes mention of this practice utilised in the United Kingdom as a means for witches to commune with the spirit world.

The third eye as a concept and working with the chakras is also a practice that is now employed by a large variant of Spiritualist Mediums as a method that makes one more susceptive the spirit world. An easy way to access this and to facilitate the use of this awareness is to keep it simple, meditate every day for ten minutes. After the ten minutes is up, focus on the centre of your forehead and visualise an eye opening up and a deep indigo colour permeating from it. If you do that daily and make time for the spirits to show you're wanting to become more aware, I guarantee you'll eventually find that your sight and hearing to the otherworld will increase, not straight away but eventually.

Gaining a Faery Counterpart

To start with, a good exercise will be to include the use of the exercise within the next chapter of this book known as: *Elphames compass round* found within the hedge crossing chapter of this work. This exercise would be best off performed on top of a burial mound, or what's known as a faerie hill. Any particular hills that have any folklore attached to them will suffice, however, sometimes it can be done on a hill that grabs you. You are to do this rite completely alone; this rite is nobody else's business but your own. Close your eyes and take ten deep calming breaths allowing your mind to go elsewhere, releasing any tension of the day, and be prepared for your journey you're about to take. Envision yourself at the foot of a silvery well, see it as a large open well that stretches down further and deeper. See the water on the mouth of this well, but as you look closer you begin to see that it has a silver cover and is a mirror.

The silvery form starts to go opaque, and you realise that this is an opening to the faery world, to Elphame's centre. You notice steps that spiral downward into the well going right to the bottom. Start to step down each step of the spiral staircase going deeper into the well, take your time. As you venture further down keep mindful that this is the shift you're taking between the world of man and the world of the fae folk. Continue walking down going deeper and deeper and once you hit the floor you see a chamber of all different doorways. These doorways lead to the faery court, the place of the King and Queen of Elphame.

Walk towards the doorway and take note of its symbols and patterns, what patterns or symbols does it hold? Is it a specific symbol? Take in the environment around you, smell, and sense the vicinity you're in. What scents can you smell? As you walk through the doorway you come to a large court hallway, there are so many people around you, these are the fae folk. Be careful not to eat or drink anything you're given here, instead politely decline.

In front of you, is the Queen of Elphame and the King of Faerie, show them reverence and respect. Remember you're in their home now, this is the courts of Elphame, and these are royalty that have dominion over it so be polite. Ask the Queen and King if they can grant you a faery folk to act as a counterpart. To act as a protector that will guide and strengthen your practice, that will run errands for you in return for offerings and protect you against any ill fae and spirits. Ask that of the King and Queen respectfully.

Gauge their reaction, if it is a no then you're simply not meant to have a counterpart. If it is a yes, then turn around and keep watchful of those around you in the court. See the crowd of the good folk standing there, from that crowd one individual will step out. That very individual is the one wishing to be your faery counterpart. Remember you will still need to negotiate with this being, make sure that you're able to offer a fair deal such as: *"If you become my counterpart and do the following, I will give you an offering every Sunday of milk and honey"*. It could be this, it could be another promise but remember to stick to your deal else it's at your peril. Walk out of the room, but this time with your counterpart and begin again to step up the stairs of the well, only this time your counterpart is there with you by your side.

Keep walking up the stairs once again, being mindful that you're leaving the world of fae and going back into the world of mortals. As you walk out of the well with your faery counterpart, you're not only bringing yourself back to the mundane world but your counterpart to the real world. So please be mindful of this, upon the hill your working is taking place at, make sure that you leave a suitable offering to the land and the fae folk including your counterpart. Milk, and honey is a traditional offering, bread, and beer, any offering you feel will be suitable for this rite before you leave to embark on your journey home. Make sure you regularly feed and talk to your counterpart once a week. Set some time aside for them.

The Alraun

The Alraun is a root that resembles a humanoid figure or holds a human-like shape to it, traditionally the root itself was that of a mandrake (also known as mandragora officinarum). However, any various type of root itself can be used just if it bears shape to a person or can be carved into a human shaped figure. Typically for this operation, the root utilised best is that of a dandelion or that of an Iris root. These are perfect and, in my opinion, it's even better if you grow these plants from a seed and watch their development as it gives you a couple of years to spend time with the plant and get to know the spirit of that root properly.

It also eliminates one of the taboos of gathering an alraun, as lore states that nobody must see you harvesting the root lest its power is made redundant. Pardon the pun, but the alraun has its roots in sixteenth-century Germany. In Hamburg in 1630, three women were said to have had alrauns about their persons and so were trialled and executed. The word 'Alraun carrier' become synonymous with witchcraft and anyone found with one was to almost be sent to the gallows.

To have an alraun was said to be a very lucky thing indeed. The alraun would ensure a myriad of different purposes such as gaining a person's love, protection for money, and finances. The water it was bathed in was said to cure cattle and help assist those in childbirth. Every Friday was said to be the day it required bathing with warm red wine or water, and lore states that if it was not fed it would shriek and create difficulty for the owner in their life.

Passing an alraun on was said to be very difficult and a way in which a practitioner would pass these familiar allies on was via another person. It was said that it could not be bought for less than what the person had acquired for. When we speak about familiar allies and familiar spirits many will often ask me, what is the way in which I can acquire one? What methods are there that bring one to me?

The Alraun is not only a familiar spirit that is documented in history and considered an actual old practice, but one that is now notorious when it comes to the reputation of the witch. Not only that, but it is also a powerful spirit ally! The root already has been a being of chthonic and literal underworldly virtues as it has been burrowed in the dark earth, whilst its plant and flowers are in the daylight. For this very reason, it's not only intrinsically linked to the otherworld, but it's betwixt.

For those wanting to acquire a familiar spirit of the Alraun, be cautious as it is a commitment but a commitment that will more than pay off as they can be worked and used within so many different operations of magic, assist you, protect you, and guide you etc. They need to be treated as a member of the family, let them know of any changes made, and keep them in the loop, they can not only grant good luck to the owner, but they can also cause bad luck. Do yourself a favour and don't acquire an alraun building a relationship with them, then toss it aside. To disregard an alraun can be a shocking error.

Acquiring an Alraun

To start with, you have two options which I will go through. The first is attaining an alraun by planting the seed of the plant you're wanting yourself. To be honest, this will take time and roughly around 2-3 years, but it is extremely worthwhile and very much worth your time if you're wanting to have an actual deeper relationship with this entity. As you will nurture its growth and development, every step of the way you will be there helping deepen your companionship together.

When planting a seed, some may perform certain rituals, but when I performed it in the past, I made sure that it was a seedling and in the succession of its beginning stages of growth, I feed it on the dark moon with some of my blood diluted by water. Leaving the seedling out in the dark moon to charge, I would at that point every Friday try and at least talk to it, or even just talk to it throughout the day. It doesn't have to be all thee and thou and mysterious invocations, it can even just be about how your day went as a whole or how excited you are to work with the spirit, or what you'd expect from the relationship in general.

Ask the spirit through this whole duration its name, this may not come straight away and may take time. It may come in a dream, it may be revealed through an omen of somebody calling out a name. It can happen in various ways but like most things in witchcraft it will happen in a way that works for yourself. Always remember though, to know somethings name is to give it power and so be wary with whom you give this name to other than yourself. If I were you, id honestly keep it a secret because there is nothing worse than placing somebody else in power over your familiar ally. Anything can happen such as the opposing witch working that spirit against you, the familiar becoming parasitic, etc.

Spirit work doesn't have to be complicated. It can be so very simplistic, and I normally find the more simplistic, the more effective it is. Every 6 months, unearth the plant being very careful not to harm the root. You can then start to lightly 'carve the root' being incredibly careful not to dig in too deep and kill the root of the plant. Make sure to carve its face, to carve its arms and legs, or any symbols or sigils you're wanting to imprint upon it. After this has been done, place the alraun upon an altar and feed your familiar ally a couple of drops of your blood along with offering two small lit birthday candles and incense of your choosing on either side just for half an hour. Once all have burnt down, bury it back into the ground.

After two years have passed, unearth the root and check on its size. If the alraun is too small for you in size continue repotting it, and occasionally carving it along with talking to it each Friday. Once the root is an adequate size for you, then buy yourself a box or even better a miniature coffin. This is used to 'bed' your newly beloved Alraun. Decorate this with symbols that mean something to you, an idea could also be to decorate the box as a traditional coffin.

It's entirely your choice, remember though this is a home for your new alraun so let them know about it! Allow them to ask what they would like in their spirit house. I'd hate for somebody to move me into a house full of sparkling tacky fake diamantes everywhere. That may be somebody else's style, but it's certainly not mine. So please be aware of making sure your spirit influences the making of this; remember it's a relationship and works two ways. Start the ritual on the full moon to the dark moon and once the root is ready, set up an altar or a place of power for the spirit to welcome it into the world.

Normally the time for me to 'birth' spirits into the world of the physical is the time of the dark moon as the full moon acts as a doorway, but during the dark moon, a time of death and the dead, the gate or door which is the moon is open. Making it easier for the spirits to come through. On the full moon, and with a working knife, take the knife and trace a clockwise circle around the plant telling the plant of your intentions that you're wanting to work with this as a magistellas or alraun. For a fully lunar month, feed the plant a mixture of your blood, milk, and water.

Main Ritual

First off make sure you will NOT be disturbed or that the ritual is somewhere where 'prying eyes' will not spot you. As mentioned, anybody else seeing such an act will render your alraun powerless. So, make sure you're doing this somewhere secluded, if you've got the plant at home in a pot, then take it indoors and close the curtains keep this between you and the spirit. If the plant is outside and you've been working with it for a while, then uprooting it on the full moon prior and carving the image you're being pulled to inscribe on the root will suffice. Traditionally, you're meant to carve the opposite sex of yourself.

In terms of transplanting the root, some may transplant this to a churchyard, but a better thing to do is to make sure that you transplant the root in a pot by your home to avoid nosey people peeking in. In the place of its absence, always make sure to leave an offering of milk, blood, tobacco, coins in the place you uprooted the alraun. Once the dark moon has come, take the plant, uproot it being careful not to damage it and trim its leaves off, and wash the root in warm water is certain to get all of the dirt off it. Tell it that you're wanting to obtain it as an alraun and in return, you will give it offerings and feed it. The traditional method is a promise to bathe the spirit every Friday but I think it's important for you to put loopholes in such as:

'I will bathe you and feed you every Friday unless I am away visiting friends and family or on a holiday in which case, I promise to let you know beforehand. In return for this promise, I want you to be my familiar spirit, to grant wishes to me, to grant good luck, to help and assist me in my sorcerous operations, to protect me against all harm, etc'

Make this yours, add what you're wanting from the spirit and remember you're keeping up your end of the bargain. So make sure you give the spirit a purpose that is going to also be worth your time. By Gods, please make sure you stick to these promises a pact is a pact, and as mentioned they really can bring a lot of misfortune if mistreated. When it comes to pacts with spirits, do not mess them about. Imagine you promised something to a dear friend, and you let them down, how upset would they be with you?

In your place of power, take the plant that was left, and form a triangle around the root, this will become the triangle of manifestation in which you will birth that spirit. Finally, take some birthday candles (as this will quite literally be the spirits day of birth) placing these around your magistellas at the three points of the triangle, lighting them. Then add a couple of drops of blood into the alrauns mouth. That night, take the alraun to bed with you as a symbol of your pact to become closer together and bond.

Once this is done, keep the alraun in its coffin until required. Every Friday wash the alraun with either warm water in a selection of herbs of your choice or bathing the alraun in warm red wine also is a method used with Madragora also known as the mandrake. As mentioned, the water used to wash an alraun can be used and worked with in healing spells, to help assist pregnancy and the delivery of children. It can also be aspersed onto the wallet, money, and debit/credit cards. Items of finance can be placed underneath the alrauns coffin/spirit house so that your money will not only be protected but also bring wealthier influences your way. It can grant wishes if the practitioner desires, the lists are endless with alrauns they are great familiar spirits to have a relationship with. However, with great benefits of a spiritual relationship, will also come great responsibility.

The Cult of the Witch: Rites and Ritual in the Old Faith

"The tradition you draw upon is native to the land on which you stand, solely because the power must ever be drawn directly through the earth where-e'er you might happen to be. The circle is the gate which opens into the earth and allows in egress through the power of the land."
　　　　　　　　　　-Andrew Chumbley The Cauldron 1995

Rituals within Traditional Witchcraft play a part but don't normally hold much organised structure as compared to ceremonial magic or more obviously the practice of Wicca. Instead, what tends to happen is more spontaneous praxis and in doing so, what tends to follow thereafter is ecstatic practices within ritual. Ecstatic experiences are when we shift our consciousness and our ordinary perception of reality and due to this, our environment changes and this is something that is often experienced when laying of the compass round or treading the mill. Both these ritualistic acts all involve the idea of shifting the world around us, causing them to become liminal spaces to connect to the spirit world and Godhead.

　　Thus, giving room for a shift in consciousness putting the practitioner in a trance-like state to perform and further connect to the working at hand. In this respect there is a myriad of exercises and instructions herein, which can not only be given as ways for the seeker to firstly engage in Traditional Witchcraft praxis, but also examples of this truly ecstatic practice that we come to know as Old Craft. For the more advanced practices of the Witch Cult, these exercises could possibly provide a way in which to add to your spiritual practice.

　　Once you lay your compass round, pretty much the ritual you perform is yours to make. You're free to completely experience your own vision and your own personal moments with the world of the spirits and any Gods or Godhead. In fact, some witches won't even lay a compass round. The following rites are structured in a way that outlines the typical features one may encounter in an Old Craft ritual and how a large majority of ritual within working groups or individuals will either follow or the structures they will incorporate but be mindful it is your choice and your practice to incorporate whatever you want.

The Clan of Tubal Cain in terms of its ritualistic practices, had a lot of influence on the structures of Old Craft working rites. I want to make it clear, that this book is pulling from different aspects and origins of Old Craft praxis in terms of the ritualistic elements of Traditional Witchcraft. The Clan of Tubal Cain is a very influential presence concerning the influence it has, so it only feels right to input some of the inspiration from the clan's ritual layouts on top of personal rituals.

It is NOT claiming to be a book that practices the exact same ways as the Clan of Tubal Cain, but to deny their influences upon Traditional Craft, would be ridiculous and unfair to the pioneers past and present that have contributed to this praxis we have today known as Traditional Witchcraft.

The Compass Round

The Compass or compass round is known by many names, the witch ring, ploughing the bloody acre, bloody furrow, etc. The list goes on and in various traditions of Old Craft just like those different geographical influences and covines within the Witch Cult, they differ. Some may state that a compass is just a Traditional Witch's version of a Wiccan circle; this is not true. In fact, it is so much more than that. Don't get me wrong, because Wicca is the most prominent of witchcraft beliefs, many think a good comparison is that of drawing differences to the practice of a Wiccan circle in order to demonstrate its differences compared to the compass of Trad Craft. A circle is primarily utilised within Wiccan covens to delineate space so that within the circle it is hallowed as sacred space ready to evoke or conjure up various Gods or Goddesses.

The Traditional Witch already sees the earth as sacred enough and so doesn't utilise the compass round for such purposes. Rather than us calling up the spirits and asking them to come to us. It is in fact US who are traversing to them, in that sense the compass round is quite shamanic in nature. I repeat shamanic in nature, I'm not insinuating that the compass round is part of a spiritual indigenous practice at all. It's just there are elements to it that hold shamanic aspects such as venturing and travelling to the spirit world. Within the compass round, we recognise six directions, four being east, south, west, and north representing spring, summer, autumn, and winter. Alongside this, we have the upper and lower world.

However, the directions or 'airts' as they are known govern different roads also. Eastward is the element of fire and the direction of spring, and the rising sun represented by the black smith's anvil, this is the direction of Tubal Cain the first blacksmith. Secondly is that being southward of the direction of earth and summers domain, it is ruled over by the Queen of Elphame, queen of the hidden folk. Thirdly is the west direction of the setting sun and autumns reign, this airt is represented by The Mighty Dead representing the waters of the dead it is also the direction of the Old One or 'Aulde Hornie'.

Now is the direction of north, the place of the northward winds and northward star, representing the gate to the Otherworld in general and the place of winter. It is the direction of Dame Fate, within a lot of Traditional Craft rituals the stang is placed here as the main altar and focal point once the compass round has been laid.

What can also occur with some covines or practitioners of the Witch Cult, also is different items can be laid in these directional places once the compass is laid to represent the airts themselves. In the east normally an anvil or a blacksmiths hammer, or iron can be placed, in the south, a bough of flowers to represent the lady in place, in the west a cauldron to represent the river of souls is placed, and last but not least in the north stands the stang representing the world tree and a medium and channel for the spirit world to pass. The word 'airt' is a Scots word which is the point of a compass or the direction of the wind. Some call the airts or direction here the four winds also, but other covines and practitioners have different names for them, it entirely depends on what works for yourself.

Most people would think that in terms of the directions, it stops with four but within the Old Craft as mentioned, there are two more to be explained. Above and below. Above represents the heavens and the ethereal world, the realm of the Gods, and the below represents Elphame itself the underworld of the good folk or the hidden folk. An idealistic symbol to represent all of these directions is that of the hexagram or six-pointed star representing the idea of the four airts, along with the heavens and the underworld, and last but not least the centre to represent the mundane world united in perfect symbolism, which represents the maxim in Traditional Witchcraft of *"all is one"*.

In history, we also see references to witches making use of circles within their practice that goes back to older times. Witches and their use of incorporating circles in their practice, isn't something that's new it's just the format and structure may have changed. I'll be the first to admit, the compass round for my practice is something that places a lot of positive impact on my practice in general and as a tool, its powerful.

You may think to yourself: by Christ, there's a lot here just for setting up a space! The truth is there isn't at all, I'm just trying to cover a large range of practices that can occur during the compass round to demonstrate the ritualistic practices of Traditional Craft.

The funny thing is, by the end of the chapter, I wouldn't have even covered them all there will be different traditions of the craft that will lay a compass round very differently, that will call in the airts differently, and will have different names for them. For example: within one Cornish tradition of witchcraft by the coven Kord Bucca, the four directions will have familiar spirits instead such as east=snake, south=hare, west=toad, north=crow.

I personally don't even really work with the airts when inside the compass round, I'm just trying to cover the basics for beginners so there's a broader understanding. Another point I'm going to add which I think is MASSIVELY important to mention is that Traditional Craft or Old Craft isn't dogmatic at all in terms of its rituals, the following methods given, are not the only way to lay a compass round.

The methods given, are not the only ways to lay a compass round, these are the methods I employ, and you do not have to do it this way. You can alter and absolutely change the layout for this rite of laying a witch ring. Some people may chant: *"throughout and about within and without"* some may not even pace about the ground and not even use tools and just use the power of their mind.

It's entirely your call, it's YOUR compass round not anybody else's it's yours. So, you do it your own way, there are many ways in order to lay a compass round, and quite frankly if I was to demonstrate many different ways to lay a compass, we would be here all day! That statement in itself demonstrates just how diverse and varied each Traditional Witch will practice. Yes, the compass in essence holds the same purpose, to travel to the otherworld, but the methods will differ greatly which is to also be applied on a broader scale for workings, spells, and charms in general. Which is what to me, in my opinion, makes the Old Craft such a beautiful thing.

For the sake of origin, I think it is so important for the seeker to investigate further into the rites concerning The Clan of Tubal Cain and their methods in which they lay the compass round. A fantastic example is given in the superb book The Star-Crossed Serpent volume one.

Personal Compass Round Rite

Bare minimum needed: Yourself, stang/broom, a glass of water, candle, or balefire, knowing the direction of north via an actual compass (most smartphones will have a compass on them.)
To begin with, take ten deep, calming, and slow breaths before undergoing this rite and state your intentions it can be so simplistic, the more simplistic the better. For instance:

"I am laying this compass round to do healing upon (full name)"

Once this is done, take three long walking circulations around three times. Now to do this you have multiple ways; the traditional way is to drag your Stang around using the forked end to 'pin down' the magic you will be casting. Another way is that of employing the witch's besom and sweeping around the perimeter. Thirdly (which is always my personal favourite) is by dragging your left foot around to form the compass round.

As this is done envision and see the ground alight glowing with witch power. I always see this as an electric blue but a colour that correlates with yourself more is absolutely fine and highly encouraged, as it makes it your own compass round. A good friend of mine when laying the compass would see it as glowing red, my cousin may see the witch ring glowing purple.

Again, it's really about what works for you. As you walk the compass round take your time and let out loud and elongated hisses really utilising that in breath and out breath with it as you go.

This represents the serpent of the land, that spiralling and pulsating lifeforce coiling throughout all the land. It is the energy of the land, the very life force itself known to the Cornish wayside witch and Cecil Williamson as 'Sprowl' the energy of the land. Once this is complete, take the vessel of cold water (the colder the better) and you're going to baptize your head, back of the neck, and your hands. This represents the traditional 'black baptism' found throughout history and lore, a way those of the Witch Cult baptise themselves to the Aulde one. As this is done you're going to say:

"I Baptise myself in the Devil's name."

Once baptised in the Crooked Ones name, a candle is lit if indoors or the balefire lit if outdoors and with this statement is given the intention:

"I light this fire in the name of the spirits of the land"

The next part is the stang being erected in the northward direction acting as an Axis Mundi bridging the world of the unseen and the seen together as they become one. The stang is placed into to ground as the witch holds the vessel visualising it as a tree bridging the two worlds together, from this point the stang is no longer just a stang, it is, in fact, a world tree, a medium that links the two worlds together. If you don't have a stang and you lived in a city where you can't walk around in the city centre on your commute to your ritual ground then, I would face the north and visualise the tree there once again acting as a bridge. Some people do use an actual tree too that too can also become an Axis Mundi, the ritual of the world tree is described during the tools section of this book.

The witch then performs perhaps in my opinion, the most important part of the rite that is integral to this tradition and its magic: speaking from your heart. So, you've said you're laying the compass to heal (full name) but why? What is the reason why you're wanting to send healing? Is she a relative? A dear friend? Somebody who is suffering? Speak from your heart, literally tell them what is happening and don't be afraid to take your time, get your emotions out, tell them how this is making you feel, etc. An example of this may seem quite mundane and down to earth but here's an example of how I do it:

"Right basically, I'm here today to heal (full name) she's a really dear friend of mine who gives literally everything to others around her and even to people she doesn't know. She has been through so much recently and now she's in so much pain with her leg. It literally brings her so much upset, and Tuesday night she was on the phone with me in absolute tears. Honestly hearing her in that much pain and misery is so hard to hear as she's done so much for me too over the years. Please spirits I'm asking you if you can help in this spell and charm to send her healing and to heal her so she can walk freely, and so that she isn't in any more pain at all. Because she is so miserable"

Not very mystical, is it? Not very jam-packed in alluring and rich deep Hollywood drama (apart from the baptism by the Devil, I'll give you that). This act of truth, simplicity, heartfelt passion, and will, in fact, DRIVES the magic to work. It will bring it from the spiritual world and into the material. That's just a wee example but honestly, see the more you go for it and open up, the more you literally pour your heart out, the ten times more potent I've personally found the working to be in general concerning the results.

Elphame's Compass Round

Elphames compass round is something I've come up with which is again in essence a compass round rite, and it really isn't that much different from the above rite at all. However, the purposes for laying Elphames compass round will differ from the latter and in fact be more introspective in nature and utilised for more internal purposes. The prime purpose of Elphames compass round is for what's known as 'fetch flight' or 'spirit flight' the travelling of the spirit. This is also known by many names such as a *toad leap into the unsee*n or a *hare leap.* You are essentially laying a compass round and preparing the ground before you in order to travel through the world via your fetch.

It very much is in essence the shamanic element that witchcraft holds to it. Again, as mentioned previously instead of conjuring up the spirits, were going to the spirits, but with this rite, it is us going to their world, which is why the following rite is perfect for spirit flight.

To begin this rite, make sure you're in a place that you won't be disturbed. This can be a secret and hidden place at night, or indoors with curtains fully shut creating an ultra-dark environment around you. Such an immersion in darkness opens up the perceptions of witch sight allowing the witch to connect and make contact with the unseen on a deeper level. The witch will then consult with familiar spirits beforehand as a means to ensure spiritual protection and guidance upon the journey to Elphame shielding and defending them from nefarious spirits that may wish you harm before taking fetch flight.

The witch will then begin to walk anti-clockwise going against the sun venturing deeper round and around envisioning and seeing them along with their familiar spirit taking steps in a downward spiral into a well. Just like the latter rite, letting out elongated hisses will help that in breath and out breath technique here, deepening your consciousness and awareness of the spirit world. You need to know and see that with each step the witch takes, they become increasingly aware of leaving the mundane world behind and that at that moment they are entering into the unseen. Take your time but see yourself eventually reaching the bottom of the well and from that point, you will light a single flame stating:

"I am here in Elphames fields in the meadows of the Goat."

Such a statement is declaring that you have reached the land of Elphame and actively travelled to the spirit world. The meadow of the goat means that this is the place also alongside the faery folk of Robin Goodfellow, Puck, Old Harry, he who goes by many names, the witch father, the Devil. From that point on, you can proceed with your hedge crossing rite, or you can also work magic within Elphame asking for its influences here. If done properly, the ritual will cause you to have strong images or see the world of Elphame around you. I have genuinely had moments where I've seen and envisioned the spirit around the circle's edge, and seen some spirits that have caused me a fright at times! However, what's important is to know you're protected by your familiar spirits and allies.

Working with the Airts or Winds

Once again, just like the compass round, there are diverse ways to bring into your compass the influence of the Airts. We work with these directional spirits to bring their influences over our workings or if were needing their assistance. For a simple way to conjure their virtues and gather their powers, we make use of the broom, or for those in the city who don't drive and aren't able to carry a broom around with them they may make use of the handheld witches sweeper; a handheld sweeper made from goose feathers originally used to sweep in and out virtues from or to the threshold or people.

Once the compass is laid, the witch will then take the broom/sweeper and will then sweep from the outside of the directional point bringing it inwards towards the compass round whilst doing an invocation. Il put the invocations here, again they can change and differ depending on different practitioners there is no dogma.

Each direction again is swept in with the broom or witches sweeper, whilst the following is muttered six times to represent the unity of the compass round and bringing those virtues inwards to them.

East

"Winds of the East, the direction of the rising sun and powers of the mighty blacksmith Tubal Cain by the rising sun, by serpents' tongue and coil come spirit by and by I call thee! Come!"

An item associated with black smithery can be placed here such as tongs, hammer, fire, etc. A traditional item placed here is the anvil. This direction can be used to rouse and raise the inner fire within, any workings to do with Tubal Cain, working with the energy of the land.

South

"Winds of the south, the direction of summer and ruled over by the blessed Queen of Elphame, by summers bough by longer days come spirit by and by I call thee come!"

A garland or bough of flowers can be placed here for the Queen of Elphame, or any other item associated with her. This direction can be worked in during workings with the Queen of Elphame and the faery kingdom.

West

"Winds of the west, the direction of the golden autumn and ruled over by The Mighty Dead, by the river of souls, by the setting of the sun, and in the name of the ancestral dead and in the name of The Aulde one come spirit come by and by come spirit."

A cauldron or vessel of water is placed in this direction to represent The Mighty Dead. A skull of man or beast to represent the Old One is placed to also represent the dead or the Devil, initiator of souls.

North

"Winds of the North, nights black majesty direction of the frozen winter and harsh cold, by the gates to the otherworld, by the threads of her known as old fate fiery creatrix of all come spirit come by and by I call thee come spirit come!"

The stang is placed as a representation of the gates to the spirit world, or thread and cord as well as a pair of scissors here can be placed to represent the threads of life and the powers Old Fate has over mortals and beasts.

The Lesser Compass

Sometimes spells and rituals don't always call for a compass round and that's ok. A large amount of the time when performing workings, I won't utilise the compass round.

When I'm doing larger rituals or I'm feeling energetically low, I will incorporate the compass round, but sometimes there can be a halfway point where the practitioner will desire to call forth a smaller version of a compass round. This can easily be done by sitting cross-legged on the floor and starting to let out once again elongated hisses, as you do this see yourself sinking downwards into the Otherworld.

Take your two hands in front of you, drawing a circle around you with both hands going the opposite direction and meeting behind you. From that point, light a candle and state the usual:

"I light this fire for the spirits of the land."

Then you're able to call any familiar spirits or any Gods you're working with or want to incorporate into the working.

Treading the Mill

Another ritual that may or may not take place after a compass round is that of what's known as 'treading the mill.' This is used to describe pacing about the compass keeping affixed towards the centre and focusing upon the central part within the compass round. Many times, chants are also inputted with this and can change depending on what kind of energies people are wanting to work on. This to the outsider looks very similar to that of raising a cone of power, a ritual in Wicca that is aimed toward raising power within a space for use via spells or charms or intentions, etc.

However, treading the mill is something that is used for raising power to a spell or working. The focus is kept in the central point of the compass round and direction of energy pointed inwards, but a lot of the time it purpose has a much more divine aspect to it.

In Traditional Craft this is done in order to connect to Godhead and the divine, and there is an incredibly beautiful account taken from Robert Cochrane which Emulates this, which was originally first published in new dimensions November 1964.

Once again treading the mill isn't an ancient or old practice, it comes from the Clan of Tubal Cain which bases its practices off older traditions and that's ok. It again doesn't take away the fact it is affective and incredibly connective towards divinity. There have been times during ritual where we've all had a group perform treading the mill and it genuinely had such an influence on me. I remember feeling the working ground spinning beneath me whilst having a beautifully intense connection with everything in the forest at the dark of night and having an awareness that all is one and that I too, am part of that. Feeling Godhead and the divine pulsating beneath my feet, feeling completely and utterly connected.

Treading the mill is a beautiful exercise and despite this book being primarily for the solitary practitioner, if you're with other people in a group setting, I would give it a try because it is something that I've found has worked pretty well. Perhaps it's all different people's energies amalgamated together working as a group unit that helps create the link to Godhead. Robert Cochrane mentions treading the mill in his letters he had written to Joe Wilson, which gives explanation as *approaching or greeting the altar* in which he stated that there is only one way to approach an altar or God stone.

What's mentioned within this, is that of mentioning kundalini energy shifting power from the spine into the mind. He also makes mention of cattle having this ability if you creep up on them, there will always be one animal with its back towards you with their head turned left or right demonstrating 'psi-power'.

He states that this is the way an altar is greeted and regards the cross of the elements which is as 'sacred to the people as the crucifix is to the Christians.' Witches dancing back-to-back, is an act that is mentioned during the witch trials as the nefarious back-to-back dance which was said to take place during sabbats. Although groups aside, it is entirely possible to perform treading the mill on your own and gain access to Godhead. I have done this and felt an incredible pull and connection afterwards from the land and the divine.

So, the purpose of treading the mill is new but as we can see it goes back to older references and if danced back-to-back has historical connections to the witch trials, confession, and records. So, if for the purpose of history, you're wanting to tread the mill this way along with the rentum tormentum invocation mentioned in the book saducismus triumphatus written by Joseph Galnvill in 1681, you would be pretty close to historical trial records of witches.

When treading the mill, I tend to just focus on the central point of the compass round walking forwards with my fingers and eyes directed towards a candle or central fire. This also works best when outside (like most Traditional Witchcraft rituals) and the central point is the balefire (bonfire).

However, this can also be used focusing upon a candle affixed between the horns of the stang standing within the centre of the witch ring.

How to Tread the Mill

Once the compass round is layed, and any workings or spells are completed then normally that's when the rite of treading the mill takes place. The group or person in a circle will start to pace around against the sun widdershins directing their energies into the balefire or candle, keeping the focus affixed upon this with the index and middle fingers stretched out directing their witch powers towards the blazing fire. At that point they start to chant, again the chant can differ, but I'll give a couple of chants here the first one is one that eventually builds up. It starts as a whisper and drags out slowly between the working group or person with slow walks and then eventually starts to build up. The walk starts to gain pace, the words become quicker and louder and louder always keeping a focus on the fire's light pacing over and over. Chanting the following:

"Rentum tormentum in the horned ones name"

Another chant that can be used for treading the mill is the IAO Formula which was introduced to me by a good friend of mine Seth David Rodriguez who is an Alexandrian wiccan. If you were looking for ancient magical formulas in this book well, I sincerely hope I haven't disappointed! It has origins in early forms of Greek Gnosticism but it is also found within different magical traditions at different points in time such featuring as one of the barbarous names in an evocation in a Greek-derived rite within the lesser key of Solomon or Goetia. Eliphas Levi mentioned this sacred formula in his book the history of magic, claiming that the formula itself appeared in ancient Egyptian calendars.

Many say that the I is symbolic of the Egyptian goddess Isis representing nature and life. The A being a representation of Apophis the destroyer representing death, and lastly, the O represents Osiris the restorer thus representing life, death, and rebirth.

The IAO is also said to be another vocalisation of the tetragrammaton an ancient name of God found in the dead sea scrolls and ancient Hebrew Aramaic texts. The tetragrammaton equates to the word YHWH (Yahweh).

Magical practitioner Aleister Crowley claimed that the name itself made up the more ancient name of Jehovah.

The actual full history of this magical ancient formula is so complexed and rich that we could again be writing another book, but its always better to give some background information of the practices in their origins and their symbolisms. I've utilised the power of this with friends in ritual, a really good friend of mine Seth David Rodriguez introduced me to this method and it's something I've found so effective within the working ritual. The chant is so simple all you do is draw out the formula and once again direct your energy towards the centre of the compass round:

"IIIIIIIIIIIIIIIIIIIIIIIIIIIIIIIIIIIIIII
AAAAAAAAAAAAAAAAAAAAAAAAAA
OOOOOOOOOOOOOOOOOO"

Phenetically this is pronounced: E I O

The Houzle or Bewitched Feast

Within a lot of animistic and spiritistic belief systems, what plays a prominent part is the giving and receiving of ritual offerings to the spirit world and the Gods. Offerings in some form or way, have always taken place between that of men and of the spirit world.

This can be found throughout archaeology within ancient iron forts, in the Bible, to the pyramids, humanity in different cultures has always found ways to give gifts to the divine and to the spirit world in its different guises. Within Traditional Witchcraft, this is no different and what we tend to do typically at the end of a ceremony is what's known as 'the Houzle'. Now there are different names for this from varying traditions, bewitched feast, red meal, troyl rite, etc. The term 'Houzle' is an Anglo-Saxon terminology for the ritual of the Eucharist.

Within different covines of Traditional Witchcraft, terminology really does vary, but ultimately the intention remains the same. It is used as a way to give the spirits thanks for their assistance during your rites, on top of this it creates a bond between yourself and your ancestors, familiar spirits, the Devil and Queen of Elphame.

It acts almost as a mass for those of the crooked path and has ties and origins within the mass itself but rather than the act of transubstantiation taking place akin to the catholic mass (the bread and wine physically becoming the flesh and blood of Christ making it the Eucharist) it is, in fact, a way in which the witch and their spirit allies and any deity they may work with becoming both linked together by both partaking the bread and wine.

The bread and wine at that point in the rite, act as a bridge between the world of the visible and invisible. Typically, the Houzle is performed at the end of the whole ritual, concluding the rite itself. However, it has been known that in some covines they perform this before as an act of welcomingin otherworldly powers with food and drink. I do understand this logic but personally, for me, the rite taking place at the end of the ritual is a way to give thanks for their presence after they've been called, and the energies and input from the spirits and Gods has been given to the working at hand. Then, the practitioner also has time to spend sitting with the spirits afterward in company listening or seeing any omens that occur after the ritual which may be messages.

It's also a time for me to ground myself by eating bread and having a sip (or two!) of wine. However, this doesn't have to be done after a ritual has taken place. The Houzle can be performed on its own as a ritual in order to bond with any household Gods or spirits the witch may be acquainted with.

Again, it can be performed differently by many different practitioners. In the Robert Cochrane letters, it is mentioned that as the clan would eat the bread, they would all groan as a group. To those in Cornwall, the witch's foot is made across the bread, it differs. I'm going to give you my version of the

Houzle that I perform feel free to add or change what you will in order to aid your own practice, as I know some witches that don't drink alcohol and so won't have it in. My cousin actually offers her favourite juice as an offering, and I've honestly worked this before with Ribena and its worked:

The Houzle Rite

To begin with, acquire some good bread or a roll. It can be homemade and in fact as previously mentioned, the more input put into the preparation the more spirits especially appreciate such efforts. Spirits especially love things that have been made by the practitioner too. It's a human-made gift, however, if you don't have time store-bought bread or rolls is fine. Another item to get hold of is wine, red wine particularly works very well as red symbolising blood and lifeforce. Once again if you make this even better but were not all vineyard owners or bakers so don't overstress if you're unable to make these from scratch.

Take your wine in a goblet and your bread in an offering bowl. Hold both hands over the items and say:

"By the Old Ones name, I hallow these items so that they will become offerings for the world of spirits from the world of men, by the powers of the underworld, by the powers of the heavens, and in the name of the Queen of Elphame, I hollow and sanctify this bread and wine. Be thou houzle!"

Take the bread and breath into it, thus breathing lifeforce into the bread and break a piece off saying:

"In the Aulde Devil's name, in the unknown fear and unknown dread, I take this oath and eat this bread and partake of him."

The bread is then eaten slowly being mindful and aware that this bread has now been hallowed and is able to connect you to the invisible world, gaining you closeness with your spirits and household Gods. After this is eaten, take the wine and then lift it up stating:

"I drink this wine in our Lady's name so that she shall gather me home again and I partake of her."

Once again, drink a portion of the wine slowly placing the awareness on the realms of spirit and your relationship with them bonding and becoming closer. Hold both hands over the bread and wine saying:

"As within so without, as above so below, I give this offering of bread and wine to the Spirits in perfect unity. May this offering and sacrifice to them deepen our relationship. Rentum tormentum in the Horned one's name!"

The offerings are left typically by a tree and the witch is to walk away and not look back through fear of undoing everything they have set out to do. However, if indoors, I tend to leave the offerings out overnight and then discard them the following morning down the sink and in the bin, as that evening the spirits will take their nourishment and sustenance from them. Many Traditional Witch books talk about leaving the offerings at a tree, which is perfect!

However, it's easier said than done when somebody lives in Manchester city centre and there are littering fines that exist. Imagine that, laying some bread and wine down for the spirits and you're slapped with a cheeky hundred pound fine, what an offering and a half! My point is, that many Old Craft books expect a witch to live right by an acre of woodland or by meadows or fields, but that's not always the case. So, when in doubt, throw it out.

Into the Night: Hedge Witchery and Fetch Flight

When we think of the witch, we often tend to have this imagery of the witch in flight usually via the use of a beast such as a goat or mounted upon a rod of some sort such as a stang, staff, or even the famed broomstick which acts as a 'steed' acting as the witches vehicle for flight the latter becoming embedded within popular culture. However, to the seeker on this path, there is an element of truth to this. The witch does in fact practice what's known as 'fetch flight' the fetch being the spirit of the witch. This is also known as many different names and can differ from witch to witch when it comes to terminologies such as hedge crossing, spirit flight, oot and aboot, going flying, or even what's known as a hare leap or a toad leap into the unseen.

The latter term being a link to animals and emitting those older folk stories of witches transforming into these creatures and being inexplicably interlinked. Within these tales, as the animal is shot or hurt by hunters, so forth is the witch themselves when seen in human form carrying the same injuries.

All these terms correspond to one practice, which is essentially the practice of the witch's fetch or spirit leaving their body and venturing into the unseen. The methods in order to facilitate such an action vary massively, but essentially it is the same thing. I want to stress that hedge crossing IS NOT guided meditation. Guided meditation is a useful tool that can help the witch to achieve hedge crossing, but ultimately these practices are not the same practice.

Guided meditation is guided by somebody else or a recording and holds a set journey for the witch whereas fetch flight your spirit is out of your physical body and you take flight into the unseen with no dictated journey, just yourself and your familiar allies doing your own journey and having your own interpersonal experiences. Within fetch flight, the witch takes their own journey and historically this can be done for a myriad of purposes:

- The witch is travelling forth due to being guided by familiar allies or familiar spirits, this is a practice seen often in witch trials.

- The witch is travelling to the Otherworld also known as Elphame to those of the wise which is essentially the world of fae or fairyland. It is said that this is the place where if one is to eat or drink, 'the good folk' will kidnap a person for seven years. Elphame is seen throughout various records, trials, ballads, and lore throughout history. However, such a journey to this place is done to meet certain spirits or to gain access to knowledge or gnosis of charms, spells, or insight into the future and this can all be done by venturing here.

- The witch can also practice hedge crossing to affect the material world around them by performing spells and charms within the Otherworld or 'Elphame'. For example, the witch can visit somebody to give them healing or the complete opposite and can send another malificia via nightmares.

- To fly and attend the sabbat; a grand meeting of witches that was said to take place historically, where the Devil himself would appear where the witch and the Old One were said to conjoin carnally, baptisms were renounced, and pacts made with spirits along with feasting, dancing, general frolics, and merriment.

I want to add, that when it comes to spirit flight there is so much history and lore attached to the witch as an ethereal being, and it's easily possible to carry on writing and I genuinely could create another book out of this and the practice of hedge witchery altogether. Adding to this, other authors have created rather brilliant books too which will be mentioned at the end of this book.

When the witch takes a hare leap into the unseen it is at that point the witch stops being 'of this world and becomes the 'other'. It is this point in my opinion where the witch gets their reputation of not fully being a physical entity within stories and never fully belonging to the corporeal. Most 'normal' people don't have the ability to allow their souls to slip out of their bodies so they're able to meet their spirit companions and travel to Elphame the land of the good folk.

It is at this point, once the witch slips out of their mortal flesh and flies into the night sky that they become of the faery folk, that they become apparitional. They become part of the invisible world. This aspect of witchcraft also known as 'hedge witchery' to many is a form of witchcraft that carries with it some deeply shamanic aspects of the Witch Cult. The shaman is a person in between this world and the other, who travels to and from the Otherworld to gain insight or knowledge from the spirit world and to sometimes collect what's known as the 'physick' or medicine for a sick or dying person.

Prior to this in-between journey, the shaman themselves will typically undergo a myriad of tests and trials from the spirit world in order to become of the 'other' to become a person standing between the two worlds. There seems to be many correlations between this idea and the idea of the witch as mentioned previously in my other book Barbarous words. Emma Wilby in her fabulous book the visions of Isobel gowdie: magic, witchcraft, and dark shamanism in seventeenth century Scotland coins the term 'dark shamanism'. The latter terminology is something to me that accurately describes this practice of hedge crossing or fetch flight.

Now, again there needs to be a disclaimer because people can have a tendency to run with things these days. I am not indicating this practice IS shamanism like what's practiced by indigenous tribes across different areas of the globe such as places like Siberia. Such a statement to my mind is deeply problematic. I'm trying to bring into context here that the practices of the witches in terms of spirit flight isn't shamanism. Hedge witchery IS shamanic in nature but isn't the same as an indigenous practice of shamanism. It would be like saying that witchcraft is fully Christian, we know there are elements of Christianity within it but that doesn't make it fully Christian. Tubal Cain technically could be classed as Christian, I don't see many of the Christian faith praying to him. it is the same situation in this context.

Preliminary Preparations

Before travelling to the otherworld, we have to be aware that much like in the realm of mortals not everyone we encounter is friendly, and unfortunately there are those that hold more sinister intentions. The exact same principle applies to the otherworld, so we need to take preliminary precautions concerning protection and warding.

Many practitioners before hedge crossing, will ask and invite their familiar spirits to accompany them on their journey or to even sometimes ask spirit allies to watch over and protect their physical body to stop spiritual invaders or parasites from entering therein. A step taken to help bring this assistance from your allies before spirit travelling, take the spirit house of your familiar and clearly commune with them your intentions: what you're setting out to do, where you are wanting to go, and that you're wanting their assistance and protection whilst placing it by the side of you.

The familiar spirit acts as a bridge between the world of the mundane and the invisible world. So it makes sense for the witch to ask their familiar spirit to help, assist and guide them into the spirit world. The familiar spirit will watch over you, they will protect you and they will bring you back.

From a physical perspective, you can also wear things on your body to protect yourself from spiritual invaders such as rowan berries and red thread fashioned into a necklace. Originally, rowan berries and red thread are mentioned in different places across the UK, as part of a folk magical practice and can have different variations to them. One such variation is taken from the book Rowan berries and red thread: a Scottish witchcraft miscellany of tales, legends, and ballads by Thomas Davidson:

"Rowan berries and red thread puts all warlocks to their sped!"

Or other variations from different places can also state:

"Rowan berries and red thread puts all witches to its speed!"

Originally, this was intended to steer away all witches and ill-wishers that would send maleficia or what's known as 'the evil eye' towards unsuspecting victims. However, despite working this charm for spirit flight, rowan berries and red thread were originally worked in folk magic in order to protect people or cattle from all supernatural harm. I can certainly attest to that. In fact, when venturing to a cemetery or a place of the dead I will often wear rowan berries upon myself as a means to protect against any 'nasties' that may have ill intent towards me. These berries can be worn around the neck of the practitioner to protect their physical body against the same negative spirits. Something I enjoy doing is creating a rosary out of those berries, along with a cross secured at the bottom made of rowan wood to double ensure its protective qualities are employed.

Another well-known protection aid is that of the hag stone. The hag stone is incorporated heavily in a lot of folk magic and witchcraft especially for ensuring protection against all harm. As well as this, they were also said to bring a person luck who stumbles upon a hag stone. It's not uncommon for those of the Witch Cult to wear a hag stone for protection but also unofficially as a symbol of their practice of more traditional-based folk magic, especially within Britain.

This aside, the hag stone is another item of power we can wear upon ourselves to protect our bodies physically whilst our spirit flies into the unseen. Roger J Horne in his fantastic book: *A Broom at Midnight: 13 Gates of Witchcraft by Spirit Flight* gives a way in which the person can employ the hag stone as a means for spirit travel. For anybody wanting to delve more into spirit flight, that would be one of the highly recommended books for a person to work with.

Another way which I was originally taught, was that of envisioning a cord around your spirit that attaches to your body's navel acting as a spiritual umbilical cord, that will always bring you back. One of the reasons I'm being so full on in terms of protection is due to spiritual parasites and spirits which may mean to do you harm as I've mentioned. Not only this, but also because your spirit can have the ability to get lost, and if it doesn't have a body to go back to then it could result in your fetch being lost in the Otherworld permanently. Take spirit flight seriously, it isn't a game, and as insightful and beautifully life changing as it is, it can have a flip side to it if the practitioner doesn't take the right precautions.

Tips for Achieving Hedge-Crossing

When discussing spirit flight, the next question people tend to ask is how does one achieve hedge riding? The witch can achieve this skill as it lies within our souls and who we are are. Traditional witch Roy Bowers (Robert Cochrane) stated the difference between a witch and a pagan is that a witch crosses between the worlds, whereas a pagan stays in this world. We're going to run through some of these methods that have been worked with historically. Alongside other methods that those of the Witch Cult use successfully to aid them in taking flight into the Invisible world.

One of the first steps to hedge witchcraft and achieving flight is accessing what's known as the 'Axis Mundi' or world tree mentioned in the tools section underneath the stang. As you will now very much know, an Axis Mundi is a medium in which the spirits travel through this tree and come to our world so it acts as a channel through which the spirits and Old Ones can come through. However, this is a two-way thing and works both ways, so it is *us* that can also travel through the Axis Mundi as a medium and spirit channel.

In order to do this, we need to go into the otherworldly geography of this place. We have the roots of the tree being the underworld and the other lower realms which many of us will know as Elphame, the land of the faery folk. The trunk of the tree for which we know as our world the world of the mundane. Lastly the branches in the tree representing the heavens being a place of the Old Ones and other lands such as what we would come to know as 'the astral realm'.

The Gods themselves aren't just attached to the upper world, there are some that you will find in Elphame such as that of the Norse Goddess Hel, ruler of the underworld will typically be found in the lower realms.

However, the world tree can be easily accessed, and the crafter can work with it as a means to travel this tree, venturing up and down its branches and roots depending on where they are wanting to proceed to. An easy way of doing this, is to lay Elphames compass round and then to perform the rite of the world tree making use of the stang or an actual tree. Once this is done, see yourself travelling up and down the tree once again. Perhaps one could even focus on shapeshifting into the form of a squirrel as a means to travel up and down the world tree effortlessly.

A key part for me personally to spirit travel also is drumming. Drumming is actually proven to alter one's consciousness and actually change someone's brain waves affecting them and slowing the brain waves to an 'alpha' rhythm. This alpha state relates to not only general well-being but also feelings of euphoria. Try it! Find a shamanic drumming track and sit or lie down in a place where you won't become interrupted and allow the rhythm to bring you into a light trance. A rhythmic shamanic drumming recording is something I use not only in workings but especially within hedge crossing. That constant rhythm creates a light trance state for me that helps shift me out of my physical shell and into the unseen.

Regarding drumming, this is perhaps within my own personal practice the most significant step that will make hedge flight successful for me. I honestly swear by it. People are different though, and again what works for me may not work for yourself. You need to find your own way, which is why I've included so many different methods for achieving fetch flight.

Another is the aspect of actually playing the drum and using this as a way to help move your spirit from your body, Many find that actually playing the drum is an act of itself for facilitating flight. Drums aren't the only instruments employed too, rattles in fact can be utilised by many as a means for again creating that constant sound that will bring to the practitioner a trance state to send them forth on their journey. Rattles have also been found by archaeologists and have been speculated that they were the main instrument used within spiritual practitioners of pre-Christian Britain during religious and spiritual ceremonies.

Another method is that of ritual tools such as the stang, as mentioned previously within artwork we see witches using the stang as a vehicle for bounding through the skies and to assist flight. This can be seen in different artworks once again as mentioned within prior chapters. The stang can be spoken to beforehand, much like the familiar spirit asking for its assistance and to be used as a vehicle and steed so that you're able to travel the unseen with it. The exact same is done with the traditional besom or broomstick. However, being honest I have used the run-of-the-mill modern-day house broom before when the traditional broom wasn't available or at hand, and it works exactly the same way! It's important for each person to find their own ways which work for them and using modern brooms is all well and good, but please don't ever let me see the day I witness someone in the other world riding to the sabbat on a Henry Hoover! This isn't hocus pocus lovelies!

Stems of ragwort, twigs, and other plants also are an incredibly traditional method for travelling to the other world. We see examples in different aspects of historical literature, such as the story known as *witch's excursion* in fairy and folk tales of the Irish peasantry in 1888 written by Walter Scott.

This story features a man named Shemus Rua, who is awakened from his slumber one evening by noises in the kitchen. When investigating these noises, he finds his old housekeeper 'Madge' sitting with a group of old crones. His housekeeper urged him to take a jug of what was known as 'posset'. An old drink of hot milk, sugar, alcohol, and lemon. Sheamus knew that once he was to take this drink it would make him deaf to the witches' antics, and so he didn't take any at all. He then went again to spy on the old women and one of them cried out, *"Is it time to be gone?"* and at the same moment, putting on a red cap, she added --
"Hie over to England!"

Making use of a twig that she held in her hand as a steed, she gracefully soared up the chimney and was rapidly followed by the rest.

Within Reginald scots discoverie of witchcraft 1584, it mentions shells as a means for the witches' steed, shells such as Cockle shells, Mussel shells, and Egg shells were said to be used for witches that would ride the sea in them:

"They can raise spirits (as others affirm) dry up springs, turn the course of running water, inhabit the sun, and stay both day and night, changing the one into the other. They can go in and out at anger holes, and sail in an eggshell, a cockle, or mussel shell, through and under the tempestuous seas."
- Reginald Scots

Because of this, often eggshells that were used were to be crushed to deter witches from creating their mischief. The latter three items that were said to be used for spirit flight weren't only just attributed to witches. They were also said to be used by the faery folk, further lessening the gap betwixt witches and the faery folk and showing them both to be beings that weren't just of in the mundane but were of the ethereal. Sieves were also said to be used too by witches acting as vehicles, in fact, this is even something that's mentioned in William Shakespeare's Macbeth act one scene three lines eight to ten:

> *"But in a sieve, I'll thither sail,*
> *And, like a rat without a tail,*
> *I'll do, I'll do, and I'll do."*

This is even seen evident in artwork such as a witch sailing to Allepo in a sieve by British artist Charles turner in 1807. As ideas, all of these are items of power some incredibly mundane that we can use as avid vehicles for spirit flight. All these items can be 'spoken' to with your wishes before travelling to the Otherworld so that they act as a steed and help facilitate the witch in their rites and workings.

Making the act of otherworldly venturing seem even more shamanic in nature, is the act of shapeshifting which is found within witchcraft and this is something mentioned earlier, that is seen so clearly in stories concerning witches and their folklore. This to me indicates the relationship between the witch and their familiar spirit or allies that act as a middleman between this world and the other world.

Not only this, but actually becoming that bestial form becomes a medium if you will for crossing the otherworld. Shapeshifting was also performed by certain shamanic cultures to take on the virtues and influences of that animal that they felt would befit themselves that they needed in the otherworld. In order to enable shapeshifting, there is a myriad of ways of accomplishing this, but a very well-known charm which once again comes from accused witch Isobel Gowdie to transform into various animals are included here, as well as the charms to transform back into human form:

"I shall go into a hare
With sorrow sign and such mickle care
And I shall go in the Devil's name
Aye while I came home again
I shall turn into a cat
With sorrow sign and a black shot
And I shall turn in the Devil's name
Aye while I come home again
I shall turn into a crow
With sorrow and sign and a black throw!
And I shall go in the Devil's name
Aye while I come home again"

In order to turn back the practitioner is to say:

"Hare hare godsend thee care
I am in a hares shape now
But il be in a woman's shape right now"

I feel like when it comes to this fabled charm, everybody gives the charm which is great as it helps keep Isobel Gowdie's legacy alive. Overall, I belive that no one really puts any experiences of actually performing the charm or even how they adapted it within modern-day rituals. I personally think this is something that should be done as it demonstrates how the charm can now be worked within a Traditional Witchcraft context and how it fits into modern praxis.

A while back, myself and a friend ventured out into a previous working place and laid the compass round, we actually at the time used something known as 'Ungeuntum Sabbati' known also throughout history as flying ointment. On top of this, we were burning various herbs and plants that added to the effect of the ointment. We stood within the compass round in complete darkness in the middle of the woods and started to sing the charm into a hauntingly beautiful song repeatedly:

> "I shall go into a hare
> In sorrow sigh, and mickle care
> And I shall go in the Devil's name
> Aye till I come home again"

This was sung recurringly, and the hairs on the back of my neck stood up in absolute delight as I felt the energy around me shift. We began to become more and more ecstatic and started to both feel ourselves lifting off the ground, almost flying. I started moving and before I knew it, I had started taking my clothes off and had laid down on the forest floor feeling completely at one with the woods in the still cold darkness.

I remember the journey well, despite not going into it fully with what I saw (as that's between myself and the spirits) I physically saw through a hare's eyes, my journey. I remember going so fast, moving amongst bushes, and even seeing certain things within the forest that on the walk back home I recognised that I hadn't paid notice to before. Once we both returned back in our bodies, myself and my friend started to move our fingers and toes and then repeated the charm to turn back obviously altered for both of us:

> "Hare hare god send thee care
> I am in a hare's shape now
> But il be in a man's shape right now"

We had both opened our eyes and had found ourselves both in our boxers but at the same time not cold and I mean it was COLD, this is Manchester were talking about here in the wintertime. What I found strange was that we had both repeated similar actions and upon talking had very similar experiences. I have to say, whilst not giving all the exact details it was one of the most beautiful moments in my life regarding my craft. Waking up and feeling the earth you work with regularly and that you have so much respect for on your bare flesh. After this was done, we dressed again, gave our offerings, and then thanked the spirits for their help, aid, and assistance.

I hope by supplying this charm as mentioned, I'm able to demonstrate loosely in what format a person can utilise and work this to fit you around you. If you're ever wanting to work this charm into a song and you're wondering how or which way to sing it, two good songs demonstrating this is Maddy Prior the fabled hare which I absolutely LOVE. Another song popular by many trad witches which is used alongside this charm is Fay Hield Hare spell.

You're probably aware but this isn't the only way of shapeshifting too. If we want to take more primal approaches, using masks to represent the animal you're wanting to shapeshift in will also have an effect and help. Alongside this, dressing yourself in the hides or skin of that animal and cloaking yourself as that particular animal or spirit helps facilitate shapeshifting. Antlers, fur, and even necklaces are all ways in which a person can take on that animalistic form, helping encourage the shifting of form between human and between beast. Dancing can be done within ritual imitating the animal's movements, if the animal jumps then jump! If the animal moves a low to the ground way, then incorporate that.

Dancing to achieve spirit flight can be a beautiful and valid way in which you physically 'take on' the animal's nature and movements before spiritually taking on those virtues. It is a way that helps prepare you and helps facilitate that.

Another method can be deprivation of sense, and this in fact can help shift the consciousness of the witch from the mundane and more towards the invisible world. When some of the senses are subdued, this can create a massive shift in mindfulness and then go on to create a deep trance-like state. In fact, Cecil Williamson mentioned the following regarding witches working in temples also:

"Locked away in this soundproof airless room, the witch working in the dim light of a beeswax candle, inhaling the atmosphere made intoxicating with heavy, sweet-smelling perfumes, soon passes into a state of trance and enters into the dream world of hallucination and ecstasy."

Entheogens

Since the very beginning of humanity, man has sorted out various methods of intoxication for visionary and spiritual purposes. The word entheogen effectively means a psychoactive substance that induces alterations in an individual's consciousness and mood for ritualistic purposes. This is found in many cultures historically and presently in the world for a very long time, as mentioned its use is ancient and witchcraft is no different.

In fact, what tends to be worked and utilised is known as 'flying ointment' a concoction of psychoactive and psychedelic plants, herbs, fungi, and other items that produce the feeling and experience of flying. It was said that witches would rub this 'ungentum sabbati' upon their bodies, take a steed, and would physically take flight.

However, one only needs to look at the ingredients to see that this meant visionary rather than taking physical flight. Flying ointment holds within it many different types of poisons, that can, in fact, kill you or cause horrific results to the body. An example is hemlock water drop, which can and will shut off your respiratory system if ingested in certain amounts. Working with poisons is no joke or not a light-hearted practice. It would be incredibly wise to seek other methods, to help assist you with spirit flight. Despite this information, I have worked with flying ointment before myself and found that it produced incredible results, I'll give an account of my experience of using flying ointment:

I applied the salve onto my skin and had all my ritual space set up along with relaxing drumming in the background and then began my ritual. I started to speak conjurations and supplications for spirit flight in a repetitive manner as I just wasn't feeling the effects at all. Eventually, after this, I gave up and started to do some meditation as a means of trying to get myself into a headspace. I still felt nothing and began to feel increasingly frustrated so declared out loud: *"This is crap!"*

That was the last thing I said, and it felt like at that point the spirits were trying to prove me wrong. I was sat crossed-legged and was physically pushed back by a force that drew me to the floor, but it was as if my head was leading me to the floor and my body followed suit after.

I didn't bang my head violently from what I remember, but I certainly remember being pushed and it felt as if I were moving in slow motion. As I looked up, I saw a large black goat over me with glaring eyes and in truth, it was a terrifying ordeal. I knew exactly who he was, his mouth opened alongside mine with sheer fright, and with that, he showed a serpent's tongue breathing into my body from his mouth.

The breath formed a mist which entered my mouth, and with that took my spirit out and I flew out. I came back, my head pounding, disorientated, and in all honesty feeling very ill. The experience was amazing, and I won't forget it, but I was very careful after that moment, to say the least! I almost felt like the moment I shouted out those three words, the spirits and Aulde Hornie himself decided to prove me wrong.

The recipe for flying ointment can be found not only in older books, but in a large number of places online. However, honestly, I would investigate other forms of methods and plant allies if need be. Look to having a glass of wine prior to the ritual or burning some loose mugwort on a charcoal block before performing your ritual to help assist you to the otherworld. Perhaps harvest some passionflower and brew it into a tea before performing a ritual to help bring you into a different mind state. Flying ointment can be bought online by herbalists that know what they're doing, but always check before buying it. Just be very careful and I can't say it enough.

Some people will also try cannabis as a means of spirit travel, and I have to say for myself it doesn't get me in the spiritual zone at all, if anything it pulls me out of it completely and attaches me to the mundane. However, I know other practitioners that have worked with this plant with great success.

We can work with plants in less dangerous ways that won't run the risk of death when using them. I do have a recipe for flying ointment but that was crafted for my body rather than somebody else's, you must understand that people have different bodies and each person's body will produce different reactions.

I am not in any way shape or form an experienced poisoner or somebody that has delved much into what's known as the 'poison path' within witchcraft. My use of entheogens within rituals over the years, has been quite a lot but I don't profess or claim that I have vast amounts of knowledge about this subject. I've been practicing for over 20 years, and I've reached a point where personally speaking as a regular practice, entheogens that can kill you aren't used frequently for me, as I'm able to access those other realms without the use of psychoactive substances.

I could give the recipe for my flying ointment but that's something I'm not going to do and to the absolute beginner with no knowledge of plants and poisons I would advise them to DO NOT do this at all. This isn't to say I don't think poisons have their place in the craft, as they really do and they are truly powerful allies that can amplify our practice in a myriad of ways. I've had truly amazing and beautiful life-changing experiences when working with magic mushrooms (psilocybin) that has changed my entire mind frame for the better. I just would not feel comfortable recommending people, especially beginners undergo working the poison path and end up permanently in the spirit world.

Chants to Facilitate Fetch Flight

Isobel Gowdie accused witch from Auldearn in Scotland, gave a charm for that of spirit flight and it is said to help facilitate the fetch travel to the invisible world. When she wanted to take flight, she was said to take wild straw or bean stalks putting them betwixt her feet saying the following charm three times:

> *"Horse and hattock, in the Devil's name!"*

Or

> *"Horse and hattock, horse and go horse and pellatris Ho Ho!"*

I will say I'm not normally very anal when it comes to full pronunciation, but please for the love of the Gods and all that is unholy make sure you get the charm right. I've often misheard it being called 'haddock' and with full sarcasm let me say, that nothing to me says spirit flight like a culinary fish dish!

Another chant taken not from a historical witch trial but from a German story in 1859 from a book known as "Der Hexenritt," *Sagen, Gebräuche und Märchen aus Westfalen und einigen andern, besonders den angrenzenden Gegenden Norddeutschlands*, Erster Theil: *Sagen* written by Leipzig: F. A. Brockhaus in 1859, uses the following charm from which draws upon the horse as the 'steed' as a means to journey out to the other world, perhaps one could chant whilst laying on the floor with their stang or broom:

> *"Horse of black, horse so fleet,*
> *Do your duty with quick feet."*

In the case of the story of Shemus and his old housekeeper Madge in the story given earlier, that when they wanted to travel over to England they would shout out:

> *"hie ho to England!"*

Perhaps such a statement could be made with the desired place and worked up as a chant over and over again as a means to facilitate fetch flight such as:

> *"hie ho to Elphame!"*
> *"hie ho to Sarah burns dream!"*

Quite often, these older tales show us methods and ways that witches ventured out into the Otherworld via spirit flight. So, I actively encourage the reader to look into other areas of folk stories and incorporate them into your craft.

Spells and Sorcery: Folk Magic within the Witch Cult

One piece of advice I would have always wanted to know and be informed about when first working in traditional folk magic based on older practices via cunning folk and witches of the past, is to go straight to the sources. By mentioning this, what I'm talking about is having a look into what books were readily available to cunning folk at the time. Such as the magus in the 1800s which influenced many cunning folk from the 1800s to the early 19th century. So, buy that very book! Get your hands on a book that has had a direct influence upon practices of the past, which in tune will have an effect on practices in the present.

Another example could be the book known as Le Petit Albert. This was made popular in France by cunning folk and wise women at the time, which is packed and full of information regarding folk magical praxis. For a practitioner living in France, the latter publication mentioned would highly give somebody an insight into the folk magical practices of France.

If in Scotland, perhaps have a look at the Carmina Gadelica by Alexander Carmichael, which was effectively a book of charms, hymns, and incantations from people in the highlands of Scotland. For somebody in Sweden, perhaps having a look at the black books of Elverum which was a black book found in somebody's attic of spells, charms, and incantations. The book has incorporated so many different bodies of influence, Christian, Pagan, and Satanic. These books are a way in which via writing the folk magic of old has become immortalized.

Have you been researching a cunning man and found out they worked with the seals from the black pullet? Then get hold of the grimoire and have a read-through! Educate yourself on the folk magic and the ceremonial magical backgrounds that have influenced older magical praxis. It is by doing this, that we are not only working magic that we can say is older spells and charms that were practiced but were also really going back to the source of what we're practicing.

One book concerning magic and its practice was a book known as the Discoverie of witchcraft by Reginald Scots published in 1584. The book is PACKED full of a myriad of spells and charms and incantations and is a great reference book for researching and delving into the early modern period Britain and its magic. An interesting and always amusing (well at least to me) story, is that Reginald Scot created this book to try to fight his case that people practicing witchcraft and folk magic, in general, were merely just superstitious, deluded, and had no power. To Scots, rather than persecuting for witchcraft, these people were ridiculous given that these practices didn't work at all, and that these harsh persecutions needed to stop because these simple people practicing magic were essentially deluded.

Reginald Scot had no idea, but what he did was secure and immortalise British folk magic by writing from 1584 onwards. He even gave various recipes and instructions for spells, charms, and enchantments which cunning folk then utilised into their magical praxis! I often wonder how he would feel knowing that today. Perhaps to some extent, it was deliberate to secretly immortalise British folk magic and witchcraft whilst trying to stop persecutions? One often wonders.

Casting Successful Spells

So, this entry is going to be different. It's not going to be comparing folklore from ages past, nor will it be looking into history in general. Instead, I'm about to give some information for the practitioner to cast successful and powerful magic. When it comes to casting, conjuring, and evoking the otherworldly powers and your own power in fact, to cause a change in the mundane world, you have to be able to fully know and believe in your abilities as well as your spirits and deities you work alongside with. That's one of the reasons why witchcraft is a path of self-empowerment.

In this day and age, the world unfortunately with the rise of human activity and mass industrialisation has become less enchanted and less magical. I'm an open person, and I honestly have no qualms in telling people I'm a witch at all. It is to me just like telling people I have black hair, I've never really had many hateful reactions from my admissions, but one of the most prominent questions I get is: "Do YoU rEaLlY bEliEvE In aLl ThAt?!" such a statement just shows and portrays how most people in the world and today's society think and where their mind frame is at.

Most people unfortunately have no magic in their lives, they haven't reached into themselves, they haven't experienced their form of power and divinity within them, and they haven't realised just how potent the world is and the power it truly holds. Of course, people have different experiences and there's nothing wrong with having different experiences and opinions. Life is a journey for most of us. However, such a reactionary statement as mentioned does radiate the general mind frame of western society.

Oh, you're wanting my reply to those questions of doubt? "Baby, I am all that." You must believe, in fact, no. Not even believe, you must KNOW that you are powerful and that at that moment you cast an act of magic, you are causing a significant effect in the world. Ignore Trevor down the road who's not got an absolute jar of glue on spirituality in general, don't let his dull, beige, closeminded way of the world dull your sparkle, and certainly don't let it affect your craft.

Your words, your intentions, your will, and your witch power will set the drive forward to cause a powerful effect in the mundane world. You must have that knowledge of your own power that in that moment, and that moment alone you have that ability. Find your power, stand firm within it and entirely own it. The other aspect of this is knowing that the spiritual world and the mundane are inherently interlinked. When we lay the compass round, by a few actions and some intent it is US that have gone to the world of spirits. The words we have, the intentions we have, and the will we have ripples out from the compass round and vibrate from the invisible world and into the world of the material. It's so important to place your awareness upon this and be mindful of it time and time again.

Many authors have called these different names such as: 'the becoming' or 'witch sight'. Witch sight to me is something I term it, but in all fairness call it what you want it doesn't matter it's about what the exercise does to your awareness and your mind. It takes you from the ordinary Joe Bloggs down the road to a witch that not only holds gnosis of their power and the powers around them, but knows how to use it effectively! That's the main part of this exercise. Like everything within the Witch Cult, there isn't a dogmatic one way of doing this at all, this is just the way I perform this working.
Available within different bodies of work regarding the craft is a myriad of ways of achieving this state, and I'm going to demonstrate mine:

The Exercise

For a start off, if you're like me and have a terrible memory, go ahead and record this exercise as a voice note on your phone in a calm and well-paced manner. Take yourself through these steps, because it is ultimately only yourself that will be able to do this. I want you to take ten deep breaths. Each time you inhale, I want you to focus on inhaling relaxation and exhaling any mundane thoughts that come into your head or may arise. Take your time in through the nose deeply, and out deeply through the mouth. Do this for ten slow counts inhaling a stillness in your body and exhaling stress.

Ten deep breaths. Once this is complete, I want you to keep awareness of your own body, and to envision yourself sitting down or laying down. Start to see sparks around your body, make this a colour that you feel particularly drawn to and that you associate with yourself. This is an exercise that's particular to YOU, no one else. This is you finding your power so by making it your colour, you're making a statement that this craft is yours and is yours alone and no one has sovereignty or say over it and never will until you allow them. You are powerful, you create change, this is your power and it is you that allows yourself to be powerful. Think of that truth lying betwixt the horns and how that piece of divinity is not only between the horns of the Old One, but also within yourself, you ARE a child of divinity.

Start to internalise that, and let that fuel sparks around you, hear the noises of the sparks around. Slowly, but surely start to see these sparks eventually turning into flames around you and start to see them spread around your body. Hear the flames cracking and growing in strength and keep thinking of the power you hold over yourself and the world around you. Start to see your witch power spread around your body like a wildfire completely taking over yourself. Burning away any insecurities and replacing them with pure empowerment.

This is your moment, this is your time, bask in your power as a spiritual being. You may feel the heat around your body, but let it burn away all insecurity and allow it to overtake you knowing your true power and recognising that piece of Godhead within you. Now keep this image going in your head of yourself encompassed by your witch powers. From this point, take your focus around you and recognise that Godhead is not only within yourself, but within every living thing and every living person. Everything has lifeforce, and a spirit and start to see webs connected to everything. All is one. All are connected by the web of Fate, the grand fiery creatrix of all.

See your fire and the energy from yourself ripple out into the world around you. Know at this moment and at this time, everything has a ripple and is attached and connected. What you do now and at this point, your words, your intentions, your actions will ripple out into the mundane affecting change where it is intended to go to. This is because everything is connected by Godhead, everything is connected by the divine and we have that ability to ripple into the web influencing our will and power to others around. Take this time to internalise this, again you may find that you feel a heat whilst doing this and even a tingling sensation. This is another way of rousing your witch fire within but more importantly, also placing your awareness around Dame Fate and the connection everything has to Godhead. It is a powerful exercise this before spell work for me is something that works brilliantly.

Within my own experience as a practitioner, a large part of spell work being successful is that of keeping shtum as they say. In other words, after casting a spell shut your mouth! Keep quiet about the working as your spell after just being cast is in a vulnerable state when it comes to others knowing about it. If you tell somebody that thinks what you do is a load of old crap, and they know you've done a spell they may take the complete piss out of it and then add those energies of doubt and ridicule into your spell work.

Once a spell works and has come to action, then by all means share away and even the methods if you want, but I normally only ever tell those close to me who are witches whom I can trust with knowing that knowledge. It's not something I'd tell Joe Bloggs on the street through fear of Joes negative and doubtful energy affecting that actual working. Remember this is your working so keep it that way! The only time an outsider should know is if it's something you've left specifically for them such as in the event of a curse, where the curse calls for you to bring awareness that they have been the target of ill intent. Such as an old East Anglian charm, which nails a toad onto somebody's door. However, with this example mentioned please don't go nailing a toad to a door as animal cruelty is animal cruelty. Perhaps a naturally found dead one will suffice, but not an alive one.

So with all this in mind, I think I could have the option to offer the reader an insight into older forms of praxis, as well as other spells that may be considered more modern but based on older lore performed by Old Craft Covens. This section could become a 'black book' of working folk magic but I think it's best to give a couple of examples on working folk magic, so the seeker is encouraged to find their journey. Once more, for anybody interested in practical folk magic then I recommend my book *Barbarous Words: a Compendium of Conjurations, British Folk Magic, and other Popish Charms.*

The Triangle of Arte

A useful tool within Old Craft practice is that of the triangle of arte, or what's sometimes known by the wise as the triangle of manifestation. Many will ask what does it do? Well, that's exactly what it does, manifest. The triangle becomes a focal point for the witch aiding them in various conjurations, charms, and spells, generally bringing more power to the workings performed.

The triangle of manifestation comes from the influence of ceremonial magic within witchcraft, and this can be seen in various ceremonial grimoires such as Goetia or the lesser key of Solomon. These grimoires make use of the triangle to contain, conjure, and bind a spirit originally via the holy names of God surrounded by the triangle. Alongside these holy names, is the name Michael representing the holy angel Saint Michael known also as the defender of God.

Typically, within the centre of this triangle, is found a crystal or some reflective image in which the spirit is seen by the ceremonial magician to commune and make contact with the celestial or infernal intelligence. However to the folk witch, the use of the triangle isn't as elaborate as that and has been adapted into the witches' rites to create what's known as a 'folk ceremonial' style of magic. This hybrid between low magic and high magic emulates older practices of the cunning folk, that is made evident within older manuscripts we have of working books belonging to wise men and wise women. An example of this are pages from the working book of cunning Murrell incorporating excerpts from the book the *magus*. It shows how adaptive the cunning folk could be and how they made something to suit their magical needs entirely.

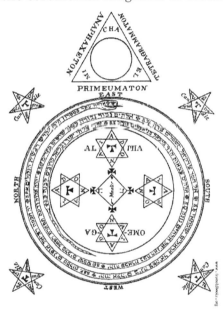

Ways in which the triangle is worked can vary from practitioner to practitioner, but the most common list of its uses are the following: Spells can be cast within it, charm bags or fetishes prepared inside, and can be left overnight within the triangle of arte to charge up in power adding more spirit force to the charm in question.

To create the triangle of arte, it can be made in a myriad of ways. It can be made from a flat piece of wood or stone that has been engraved by the practitioner. A simplistic option, is to take three sticks equal in length and bind them with natural twine to make a natural triangle and worked this into their magic. The triangle can even also be inscribed or drawn onto the floor with chalk/liquid chalk, bonemeal, or when the practitioner is in the woods, it can be drawn on the working ground with the stang or working stick to take part in the crafter's ritual.

Some people will also vary the different types of wood they use, to bring in different virtues those woods will be associated with. For example for cursing or the malefic intent of 'blasting' blackthorn will be used, for wisdom; oak, for love; willow, for healing; birch, for strength and protection; holly or rowan. The list goes on and depending again on what virtues and powers are needed, the world is your oyster.

Sometimes the triangle can be drawn or inscribed upon a working altar or working table placed with the holy names of God around it such as 'tetragrammaton' so that when conjurations take place, everything is done within that triangle.

The triangle is a powerful symbol, holding the number three into a shape. Throughout history the element of three has always played a part in magic, land, sea, and sky. Mother, maiden and crone. Father son, and holy ghost, etc. The symbol of those triple virtues being inputted into your magic, is a powerful ally to have to raise that energy and those intentions. What's included here as a picture is an illustration taken from the lesser key of Solomon by MacGregor Mathers bearing the triangle of manifestation. At the very top of the diagram, is that of the triangle of arte, and below it is the circle in which its purpose is originally used for.

The Nine Herbs Charm

This older charm known by the Anglo Saxons as the 'nine herbs charm' was found in a medical manuscript in the late tenth or eleventh century known as *Lacnunga*. The following charm is used for eliminating poisons from a person and curing them via the use of the nine sacred herbs. Originally the mix of herbs was to be spoken the charm to, and then compiled into soap and used to draw out toxic poisons. This is mentioned as such:

"Mugwort, waybread open form the east, lamb's cress, atterlothe, maythe, nettle, crab-apple, chervil and fennel, old soap; pound the herbs to a powder, mix them with the soap and the juice of the apple. Then prepare a paste of water and of ashes, take fennel, boil it with the paste and wash it with a beaten egg when you apply the salve, both before and after. Sing this charm three times on each of the herbs before you prepare them, and likewise on the apple. And sing the same charm into the mouth of the man and into both his ears and on the wound, before you apply the salve."

However, a more modern way to perform this charm could be to utilise these herbs and use them for healing specific ailments on a client, or if you feel there need to be different herbs in there (such as boneset for healing bones) then go ahead and incorporate this into the charm instead! Another aspect is rather than compiling an actual salve, the herbs after being spoken to, could be placed around a candle in a circle, with the client's name inscribed within the centre, along with somebody's personal effects. A modification of the charm for flu could be:

*"And you, waybread, mother of herbs,
open from the east, mighty inside.
Over you chariots creaked, over you queens rode,
over you brides cried out, over you bulls snorted.
You withstood all of them, you dashed against them.
May you likewise withstand influenza and illness
and the loathsome foe roving through the land."*

Such an alteration of an older charm is favourable especially when concerning long distance healing sent to a client or a poorly loved one.

The Charm

Nine herbs: Mugwort, plantain, lambs' cress, nettle, betony, chamomile, crab apple, thyme, and fennel.

> "Remember, Mugwort, what you made known,
> what you arranged at Regenmeld.
> You were called Una, the oldest of herbs,
> you have power against three and against thirty,
> you have power against poison and against infection,
> you have power against the loathsome foe roving through the land.
> And you, waybread, mother of herbs,
> open from the east, mighty inside.
> Over you chariots creaked, over you queens rode,
> over you brides cried out, over you bulls snorted.
> You withstood all of them, you dashed against them.
> May you likewise withstand poison and infection
> and the loathsome foe roving through the land.
> 'Stune' is the name of this herb, it grew on a stone,
> it stands up against poison, it dashes against poison,
> it drives out the hostile one, it casts out poison.
> This is the herb that fought against the snake,
> it has power against poison, it has power against infection,
> it has power against the loathsome foe roving through the land.
> Now, atterlothe, put to flight now, Venom-loather, the greater poisons,
> though you are the lesser,
> you the mightier, conquer the lesser poisons until he is cured of both.
> Remember, maythe, what you made known,
> what you accomplished at Alorford,
> that never a man should lose his life from infection
> after maythe was prepared for his food.

This is the herb that is called 'Wergulu'.
A seal sent it across the sea right,
a vexation to poison, a help to others.
It stands against pain, it dashes against poison,
it has power against three and against thirty,
against the hand of a fiend and against mighty devices,
against the spell of mean creatures.
There the Apple accomplished it against poison
that she [the loathsome serpent] would never dwell in the house.
Chervil and Fennel, two very mighty one.
They were created by the wise Lord,
holy in heaven as He hung;
He set and sent them to the seven worlds,
to the wretched and the fortunate, as a help to all."
"These nine have power against nine poisons.
A worm came crawling, it killed nothing.
For Woden took nine glory twigs,
he smote the adder that it flew apart into nine parts.
Now, these nine herbs have power against nine evil spirits,
against nine poisons, and against nine infections:
Against the red poison, against the foul poison.
against the yellow poison, against the green poison,
against the black poison, against the blue poison,
against the brown poison, against the crimson poison.
Against worm-blister, against water-blister,
against thorn-blister, against thistle-blister,
against ice-blister, against poison-blister.
Against harmfulness of the air, against harmfulness of the ground,
against harmfulness of the sea.
If any poison comes flying from the east,
or any from the north, [or any from the south,]
or any from the west among the people.
Woden stood over diseases of every kind.
I alone know a running stream,
and the nine adders beware of it.
May all the weeds spring up as herbs from their roots,
the seas slip apart, all salt water,
when I blow this poison from you."

Dark Moon Bread Poppet

In the practice of witchcraft, the use of dolls and nefarious insertion of pins, glass, and other sharp objects have created a deadly reputation in which most associate with the art of witchcraft. There are many ways to create an 'image' or 'poppet' as they are known, one of the most destructive and feared techniques is that of employing the use of bread to form a representation of the person. Not only is Bread used with this because it rots away, so in this instance its best to work for baneful magic of sending ill intent towards an intended target, but it is employed because it contains all four elements. The bread mix is earth, the water you add to the mix is used, the fires of the oven are used and lastly the bread itself rises which is a representation of air.

The following rite is inspired heavily by a well-known You tube video ive seen over the years by a channel known as DorsetWildlifeRescue. They have an array of beautiful videos concerning the protection of wildlife featuring the release of endangered animals such as the Adder or European viper, they do a lot of good for the wildlife they protect and help preserve. Another aspect of their videos are that of their coven *Cauldron of the Alta Cailleach*, in which they demonstrate various methods of witchery. One such video is labelled 'Lilith's Dark Moon Poppets' which this working is inspired by a significant amount.

I'd like to share this as I think it helps preserve the legacy of these videos and their descriptions. As a disclaimer please be aware however, that the ingredients worked into this are incredibly poisonous, so please be extra cautious. Another aspect here is that during the whole process, fixed intent must be set onto the intended target the whole duration of the spell. On the Dark Moon, start with some bread mix store bought is completely fine and into this burn the ashes of the persons full name and their date of birth. Start to add water mixing and kneading the bread, from this point you're going to add ground up baneful herbs into this plant such as the following: Mandrake, Belladonna, Valerian root, Yew leaves and lastly dirt taken from a Grave. Stirring anti-clockwise or widdershins being sure to talk to each ingredient asking them to bring baneful intentions to your targets life. Then mix this powder into the bread mix, and start to fold in into it. At this point, vinegar is added to 'sour' the dough and make to it bitter.

Form the dough into the person you are intending to target and try to be as detailed as possible, including trying to be as accurate as you can on their body parts and genitals. Etch their name into your poppet across the body, and where the mouth of the poppet is, make a small opening, breathing into it envisioning and seeing a part of that person's essence becoming linked to the poppet. From this point, the poppet is put into the fire to be baked, and once done the poppet can be struck with blackthorns, glass, sharp objects in various areas to inflict a various number of maladies.

To Prepare a Love Potion

"The following substances must be gathered in silence when the full moon is in the heavens: three white rose leaves, three red rose leaves, three forget me not, and five blossoms of veronica. All these things you must place in a vessel then pour upon them five hundred and ninety-five drops of clear easter water. Placing the vessel over the fire or better still over the spirit lamp. This mixture must be allowed to boil for exactly the sixteenth of an hour. When it has boiled for the requisite length of time, remove it from the fire and pour it into a flask. Cork it tightly, seal it and it will keep for years without losing its virtue. That this potion is certain in its effects I will guarantee for I have gained more than thirty hearts by its help. Three drops swallowed by the person whose love you desire will suffice."
Golden wheel 1862

I'd like to add to this potion a little bit. With all due respect, and in my opinion, sometimes these exact drops and measurements and even boiling over a fire can be a bit pedantic. Sometimes gathering the plants in silence, and using dried parts in silence, then filling the vessel with the easter water, and boiling it on the cheeky stove for 16 minutes will do just fine!

Cecil Williamson the Go Away Doll

An interesting working of folk magic demonstrated by Cecil on the 1999 channel 4 programs known as 'far out' featured himself cradling an image or a doll and using what's known as his 'humming magic'. He describes a doll that was made of a villager who was a *'pain in the neck'* and so because of this, less aggressive acts of magic would be employed as opposed to striking the doll with pins or burning the image. This humming magic involves the doll being rocked back and forth with both the hands, chanting and droning out words of taking leave such as:

"Goooooo awaaaaaay awaaaaaaaay awaaaaaaayawaaaaaay awaaaaaaaaaay leeeeeeave leeeeeeaaaave leeeeeeaaaave leeeeeeeeeeaaaaaaaaaave leeeeeeeeeaaaaaaaaave don't staaaaaaaaay do not staaaaaaaaaaaay do not staaaaaaaaaaaay."

The action was said to be carried out for 2 hours at the least, in order to make somebody take flight away from the person who no longer desires their presence.

To Stop Your Man from Being Attracted by Another

According to English folklore by Arthur Robinson, a woman in Norfolk discovered her husband was attracted to another woman. By a friend she was given the Lord's prayer written backwards, which she had fastened under her blouse and kept there for three days each week until her husband's curiosity ceased. After a Fortnight, he didn't even recognise the other woman. For a man doing this, I imagine the same would be done but fastened under your underwear.

Image Killing the Charm Known as 'Burn the Witch'

To combat ill witchcraft and misfortune sent to one, there is the following spell supplied by the book Golspie, contributions to folklore collected by Edward Williams Byron Nicolson in 1897. The following charm was created by an old woman 'well versed in the ways of witches' who after having been supplied silver by an unlucky family plagued with misfortune, told the family to meet them outside the house at midnight. There, a fire was built and lit before the house as the family all joined hands and stood in a circle. Meanwhile, the old woman carrying a crudely made rag doll stuck full of pins walked to the fire and muttered some words of power, and threw it into the fire. As the image of the witch was burning, the family danced around the fire screaming and shouting at the top of their lungs until the image of the supposed witch succumbed completely to the fire.

The Witches Eucharist

The Holy Eucharist to those of the catholic faith, is a wafer alongside wine representing the body and the blood of Christ. At a certain point within the mass to those of the Catholic faith, the bread and wine are said to physically become the actual embodiment of the flesh and the blood of Christ. This has an actual name known as 'transubstantiation' this occurrence isn't just something that is held in spiritual value to Catholics.

To those of the Witch Cult, the eucharist holds within it power that has historically been worked with.

Examples can be seen throughout different lore throughout the ages. An example well known within the lore of the craft, is that of a ritual that initiates the witch onto the cunning path. This involves the witch stealing a communion wafer during mass and at midnight they were to return to the churchyard. There, in the black of night the witch was said to go around the churches perimeter widdershins repeating the lord's prayer backward three times. Upon the third time, the witch would be met with a toad, open-mouthed and ready to receive the stolen host. The host would be fed to the creature and the toad would then breathe upon the witch three times, and it was at that point the witch would be initiated into the black arts.

What's interesting, is that toads have an alliance with witchcraft throughout various lore and tales told by those of older times. The toad is said to be a representation of the Aulde one himself, as the Devil's coat of arms was said to bear upon it three toads. In Normandy between 1585-1630 witch trials (in which a large demographic were men) practitioners were said to utilise toads in a way to create what's known as 'toad venom' which would injure and create ailments in people.

However, to witches in Normandy, it was said that the most powerful benevolent magic required the stolen host once again. This act not only represents the Luciferian aspect of old folk witchcraft but represents the 'dual faith' aspect of the Old Craft too showing the incorporation and power within the Christian spiritual ecology.

The wafer itself can also be fed to a familiar spirit ritualistically and inputted into a balefire during ritual to represent it being taken in by the otherworldly powers gaining even more potency and power to a familiar spirit. In fact for large tasks, promising the familiar the host as an offering in return does have its benefits.

However, once again always make sure that you do attain the host and feed it to them in return for their more arduous tasks as a part to keep up that promise. The stolen host can also be added to charm bags or to spells, particularly when it comes to benevolent magic to amplify the power of the workings. Another charm utilising the Host, or at the very least three, to cure one of the fevers is found within *the book of witches* written by Oliver Madox Hueffer written in 1922.
Take three holy wafers and write on the first: "So is the father, so is life"; on the second, "So is the son, so is the saint"; on the third, "So is the holy ghost so is the remedy." Take these three wafers to the fever patient and tell him to eat them on three consecutive days, neither eating nor drinking

anything else; also say fifteen times daily the Pater and the Ave.

"A witch is born, and not made;
or if one is to be made then tears must be spilt before the moon can be drawn. For the Lady chooses whom She wills to be Her Lover, and those whom She loves most She rends apart before making them Wise."

— Robert Cochrane

Conclusion

I hope by reading this book the seeker has gained an understanding of Traditional Witchcraft, not just its actual practices but its origins which is something I deeply craved for more understanding about when I was embarking on this path. It's part of an inquisitive nature we as humans have, where does this come from? Who was it that gave the basis for these practices? Where do its origins lie? In truth, this book has been easy to write unlike my first book barbarous words, but it's made me realise just how much I could have kept on writing when it comes to the origins as well as general practices within the Old Craft system.

Because the nameless art is so vast with its different practices, I could have continued writing on the different branches of Traditional Witchcraft be it more aspects of Cochranian tradition, Sabbatic witchcraft, hedge witchery, the regency, etc. The list of branches within Traditional Witchcraft vary greatly.

That's why within Traditional Witchcraft as much as we may have similar rituals such as the compass round, as mentioned how we cast the compass round will differ from varying traditions. It's important to be mindful of this when researching and reading up on the Old Craft, especially for the first time. In that sense, concerning its structures and spontaneity, it is not like traditional Wiccan systems such as

Gardnerian and Alexandrian Wicca where there tends to be a more set structure.

I could also write about different aspects of the craft, there have been so many books written over the years dedicated entirely to specific aspects of the craft. The point is, in this book the ineffable name; I hope that I have portrayed what's known as 'the bare bones' of praxis as well as some of the origins and structure of the craft in which is practiced. All in all, I hope I've achieved this goal within this book as well as hopefully inspired some of you when it comes to forming your practice, remember it is nobody else's witchcraft, it is your way.

By indicating I could continue writing, instead what I am trying to portray is that Traditional Witchcraft has so many different bodies of influence that have affected it that there will still be things within this book I will miss. Which in actuality, points out the beauty of it as a tradition, the beauty that so many people from different places have had an effect upon this tradition and that in effect.

Traditional Witchcraft has become a vast melting pot, forming together the old and new to create and give birth to a not only accessible but beautiful practice. It is this very practice, that has to lead me through my life with experiences and the continuation of gaining knowledge that will certainly never leave me and will stay with me until the moment my number is up and I'm called back 'home again' to the spirit world.

This brings me to the next section and in fact, the main section, which mainly concerns you doing you and il get into what this means. We live in such a judgemental world, to the point many others suffer in the world and have done purely for being different or not fully fitting into mainstream society, this is seen in really damaging ways throughout history and the modern day. Within your life, no matter what you will do, somebody will comment or make critical mentions of quite frankly something that doesn't concern them at all, and this is no different when it comes to your practice.

I've been a practitioner for over twenty years as mentioned, and my whole life I've experienced criticism from society alongside those within the magical and occult community. Most criticism has made mentions of the way I practice and the things I believe in as a system of magic and spiritual worldviews that fully fulfills every fibre of my being. I've got news for you, these people be they non-magical people (what's traditionally known as 'cowans') or be they those of the magical community it doesn't matter, what matters is that you are doing you. That you are practicing something that connects you to Godhead and that you have a personal connection to the spirits and that ultimately the craft you practice works.

As long as you're not hurting anybody (within reason, we discussed hexing and cursing in the introduction) all that matters is you have a connection to Godhead and access to powers otherworldly that can affect the change in the mundane world. It was Andrew Chumbley who mentioned the following quotation which I've used for YEARS in my practice and its beginning to become a personal joke how often I say it, but I cannot fault it:

"If somebody knocks on the door and the Gods answer, then who I am to question the integrity of their path?"

It's a quote that I've internalised within myself alongside another quote coming from the practice of Thelema; a system of ceremonial magic by Aleister Crowley: *do what thou wilt.* Many think this is a free for all as in do whatever the hell you want, but one only needs to look closer to recognise that this isn't what this fully means. Your will essentially is what you're meant to do, i.e., your Fate the reason you are here on this planet, and finding that, doing it and being good at it. Despite this again not being attributed to the Old Craft current of belief system, it is something that for me is heavily embodied into my mind frame for the exact reason of being a witch.

Being a witch whether by birth or by later discovery is something that you are. It is like having brown eyes or being a certain sexuality, it's ultimately nothing that you choose to be, it's something you are by nature. Now that doesn't make you more special than anybody else, some people are great plumbers, some people are talented artists or dancers, and some people are good witches. If you are naturally a witch whether brought up with it, or it's something that's discovered it is something that you naturally are. You cannot change it, the spirits and Gods in my personal belief choose witches, as we stand betwixt everything, we are liminal creatures standing in the world of the mundane and the world of spirits, and in doing so we do not belong fully and sadly never will as such is the way of the witch.

This is part of our will, part of our destiny to realise and know who we are, and part of your will is to do you and be good at it. There will be those who will criticise and even condemn, those who will run a mile, and those who will treat your differently if they know of that aspect of who you are. Some people will also jest and take the downright piss about yourself and your practice, I've had times when even in places I've worked I've requested my holidays off for the sabbats and people have looked at me and said: "that's not a real reason, it's not even a real religion or serious thing". Such a statement is ridiculous, our belief is as justified as any other religion or spirituality going. Whilst people who practice witchcraft are accepted ten times more as compared to the early modern period, we're still ridiculed and criticised for what we do and for our beliefs.

Some people stay in the broom closet i.e.: not telling everybody or letting only a few people aware of their spiritual practice. However, some are unapologetically open and that's my take on things. The way I see it, I shouldn't hide who I am from anybody or even change a portion of myself, a portion of myself that has quite frankly saved my life multiple amounts of times. Witchcraft has stopped me from being homeless, it's allowed me to make last-minute decisions like moving cities and country with no job and being able to secure a flat and a job. It saved my emotional health, and it showed me how much of a powerful human being I am and helped me reach my full potential. It has revealed to me the powers and very existence of the spirit world itself.

It is done so much more than this hence the title of the book: *the ineffable name.* Something too great to even put into words or begin to describe. What witchcraft has done for me is so much more than words could ever explain so why oh why would I change myself for somebody's approval I don't even know. I need nobody's approval in this life of who I am but my own, and that's something to internalise.

Of course, a practitioner doesn't have to be as blatantly open as me or run down the road with some sort of witch pride parade. I guess what I'm trying to say is if you do have an encounter with somebody not approving (which you will at one point of your life) just try to be mindful of the above and that's why the following quote by the witch of kings cross Rosaleen Norton speaks to me incredibly:

"I do not wish to propagate any cult, even the Witch Cult, change society, or establish a better world for others. These things leave me entirely indifferent. I have what I describe as a function, the function is that of focus and catalyst. And this function is best served by me performing my own personal will and not caring a damn about effects good or bad on people."

For those of you who may not be familiar with Rosaleen Norton, she was an artist known as the witch of kings cross during the 1950s in conservative Australia. She was unapologetically herself and despite all the awful treatment such as being arrested, having her home broken into multiple times by the authorities, books banned, and artwork destroyed. She endured through her beliefs and artistic expression as well as her unconventional life at the time which let's face it, if it's behind closed doors and not hurting anybody its nobody's damn business but these were different times.

Despite all of the persecution she faced, she carried on fulfilling her will and was a resilient character. For me, it is people like her who inspire me to truly be myself and to carry out part of my 'will' of being a witch. For anybody wishing to know more about Rosaleen Norton and the incredibly interesting life she lived, check out the documentary the witch of kings cross directed by Sonia Bible on amazon prime. It's an inspirationally fantastic watch, as well as this check out her artwork it's incredibly beautiful and thought-provoking, to my mind it shows she was in contact with the spirit world too.

Another character who was resilient and has been mentioned throughout was Cecil Williamson with his earlier known' witchcraft research centre' which we commonly have come to know as the museum of witchcraft and magic in Boscastle.

Had he not done this and created the museum, a large majority of artifacts we have about folk magic (particularly in Britain) would have been wasted away in the seas of time and lost. Many people call him the unsung hero of folk magic and Traditional Witchcraft as he single-headedly preserved a lot of folk magic and Traditional Witchcraft ways. Despite his efforts at the time, he was faced with a lot of persecution and had to move his witchcraft research centre five times across different places from the Isle of Mann to Cornwall. He even had windows smashed in, and was faced with threats of death, and had been threatened by the local village priest who shortly after the confrontation with Cecil, had taken ill and suffered a heart attack.

Such characters throughout history being the fathers and mothers of the development of what we now come to know as modern practices and forms of witchcraft, really were in most instances completely and utterly themselves. They didn't budge or change for anybody, rather than it was only themselves who they embraced. Being a bit of an anti-authoritarian myself there is something I find not only inspiring but beautiful as during that time of ultra-conservative attitudes, these people stuck their middle fingers up as a final 'fuck you' to general society refusing to convert to the way society expected them to be. Rather than this, they realised they were to be their true selves and if society had an issue with it then that is ultimately an amplification of society rather than the individual being targeted. Such is the way of the witch, not to fit in directly because they are being their true selves. This to me I find completely enlightening and not only brave, but beautifully defiant.

Not only does a practitioner new or experienced have to undergo a bit of grief from those who are non-initiated in the craft, but they may experience some criticism from those who practice also! It is unfortunately not uncommon news that witches throughout the ages don't always get on with each other and this stands regarding personal beliefs and practices when it comes to the craft in general. This is something we've seen through history too from the case of the Pendle witch trials between the Demdikes and Chattox to the more modern forms of witchcraft such as Cecil Williamson and Gerald Gardner.

I have unfortunately experienced the toxic side of criticism. Where other practitioners will try their best to demean you or even put you down when it comes to your practice. Years ago, when I was seventeen, I had somebody do exactly that and reduce me to absolute tears, criticising my practices and my methods in a spiteful way that was completely uncalled for. I'll never forget how spiteful the individual was especially me being so young and themselves being older than me, but you live and learn. The lesson was to not let anybody dull my sparkle and if it concerned my practice then it didn't concern them at all and had diddly squat to do with other people. The fact is some people can be nasty, but ultimately their critics aren't usually of you it's a sad mirror image of themselves.

By them trying to actively put you down, they are actually in tune trying to camouflage their insecurities in general so that you become the scapegoat for such insecurity. Do not feed into people like this, even if they say anything appalling or horrific, do not invest energy into actively toxic people, as the only person you will end up hurting is yourself. When it comes to personal practice, and somebody is slating down my practice or things that I do, I always internalise the fact that; when it comes to my witchcraft, the only people I have to answer for are my spirits and Gods which I work with that's all. Not toxic Thomas and his narcissistic small man syndrome, I just have myself and the spirits to answer to. Life is too damn short for investing in negative energy when you could be investing energy positively to yourself and your practice and not allowing negative people to affect you. In truth, it riles them up more, but ultimately and more importantly it's much better for you and your life.

Like it or not, there will be some practitioners that unfortunately feel the need to criticise your practices and this can be for a myriad of reasons but sometimes it can come from a good place, such as yourself not having any awareness of where something comes from and claiming it as your own when it's not from your tradition at all. An example of this would be practicing a hoodoo charm and spell and calling it 'Traditional European witchcraft'. Such a statement is a bit troublesome as hoodoo has its history and own practice and to claim that tradition just like 'traditional European witchcraft' shows little or no respect to that tradition and its history. So a healthy dose if criticism is helpful and does have its place.

The relationship you have between yourself, your spirits, and Gods has absolutely nothing to do with anybody else apart from you. Nobody should dictate how you practice and what you practice, it's your practice and your choice. The exact same sentiment applies to your life in general too. Make it your own and own it. After all, witchcraft is a spiritually nourishing path that strives towards self-empowerment.

However, with the aforesaid mentioned, not everybody is out to attack you, people are there to also help you and inspire you, and be open to what others have to say as they can and will at times benefit your practice greatly. There will be those around you who may be other witches with whom you can create a small working group together even a coven. You can also learn a lot from other witches' practices and that doesn't just stay at only Traditional Witches. Witches from other traditions are also good to have around as friends, as you learn a lot about other forms of witchcraft and maybe even become inspired to incorporate or research further into other traditions.

Whilst writing this book it's been an incredible journey for me, not just in terms of writing but whilst I've been practicing too. It's made me realise just how lucky I've been throughout the years having gained those experiences, and remembering moments that I believe will stay with me for the rest of my life. I sincerely hope that the newcomer to witchcraft experience similar encounters that I have had and that they find ways to connect to the spirits, to Godhead, and ultimately to know themselves and become empowered by that.

I hope that by working the methods of praxis within this corpus of work regarding the arte, this achieves these things and If this book can honestly allow even just one person to undergo these moments of experience with the Old faith, il be a happy man. With that, I'll end the book on the following old Saxon blessing mentioned by Roy Bowers (Rober Cochrane): Flaggs, Flax, Fodder, and Frigg. May you have clothes on your back, food in your bellies, a roof over your head, and somebody to love.

Recommended reading and Bibliography

Agrippa, Cornelius, *Agrippa four books of occult philosophy.* 1531

Baker, Jim, *The cunning man's handbook.* 2014

Barett Fraancis, *The Magus.* 1801

Campbell, Gregorson, *Witchcraft and Second Sight in the Highlands and Islands of Scotland.* 1902

Chambers, Ian, *The Witch Compass: Working with the winds in Traditional Witchcraft.* 2022

Cockayne, Oswald, *Leechdoms, Wortcunning, and Starcraft of Early England.* 1864

Cummer, Veronica, Robin Artisson, Christopher Crittenden, Nicholaj de Mattos Frisvold, Eric de Vries, Rev. Jack Green, Raven Grimassi, Beth Hansen-Buth, Juniper, Sylva Markson, Jenne Micale, Papa Toad Bone, John Pwyll, Elige Stewart, Kari Tauring *To Fly By Night: The Craft Of The Hedgewitch.* 2010

Davies, J, Hubert, *The Silver Bullet and other American Witch Stories.* 1975

Davies, Owen, *Popular magic.* 2003

Foxwood, Orion, *The Flame in the Cauldron: A Book of Old Style Witchery.* 2015

Froome, Joyce, *Wicked enchantments a history of the pendle witches and their magic.* 2012

Gary, Gemma, *The Black Toad.* 2012

Gary, Gemma, *The Devil's Dozen.* 2015

Gary, Gemma, *Traditional Witchcraft a Cornish book of ways.* 2008

Gary, Gemma, *Silent as the Trees: Devonshire Witchcraft, Folklore and Magic.* 2017

Grace, Christine *The Witch at The Forests Edge.* 2021

Hares, George, *Barbarous Words: A Compendium of Conjurations, British Folk Magic, and Other Popish Charms.* 2021

Howard, Michael, *East Anglian witches and wizards.* 2017

Horne, J, Roger, *Folk Witchcraft: A Guide To Lore, Land, and The Familiar Spirit for The Solitary Practitioner.* 2019

Horne, J, Roger, *A Broom At Midnight: 13 Gates of Witchcraft By Spirit Flight.* 2021

Huson, Paul, *Mastering Witchcraft: A Practical Guide For Witches, Warlocks, and Covens.* 1970

Jackson, Nigel, *Call of the Horned Piper.* 1994

Jackson, Nigel, *Masks of Misrule: The Horned God and His Cult in Europe.* 1996

King, Graham, *The British book of charms and spells.* 2016

Mercer, Andrew, *The wicked shall decay.* 2018

Mercury, Kelden, *The Crooked Path: An Introduction to Tarditional Witchcraft.* 2020

Nicholson, Edward, *Golspie: Contributions to Its Folklore.* 1897

Oates Shani, Evan John Jones *The Star-Crossed Serpent Volume 1- Origins: Evan John Jones 1966-1998 The Legend of Tubal Cain.* 2012

Oates, Shani, *The Star-Crossed Serpent Volume II The Clan of Tubal Cain Today: The Legacy Continues.* 2012

Oates, Shani, *The Star-Crossed Serpent III: The Taper That Lights The Way: Robert Cochrane's Letters Revealed.* 2016

Oberon, Aaron, *Southern Cunning: Folkloric American Witchcraft In The South.* 2019

Paddon, Peter, *A Grimoire For Modern Cunningfolk a Practical Guide to Witchcraft on The Crooked Path.* 2010

Pearson Nigel, *The Devil's Plantation.* 2016

Pearson, Nigel, *Treading The Mill.* 2007

Rankine, David.ed, *The Grimoire of Arthur Gauntlet: a Seventeenth Century London Cunning Man's Book of Charms Conjurations and Prayers.* 2011

Saille, Harmonia, *Pagan Portals: Hedge Riding.* 2012

Scot, Reginald, *The Discoverie of Witchcraft.* 1584

Singer, William, *an exposition on the Miller and Horseman's word or the true system of raising the devil* 1881

Wilby, Emma, *Cunning folk and familiar spirits.* 2002

Wilby, Emma, *Visions of Isobel Gowdie: Magic, Witchcraft, and Dark Shamanism in Seventeenth Century Scotland.* 2010

About the Author

George Hares is a practicing Witch, British folk magician, and Root Worker located in Paisley, Scotland. He is the author of Barbarous Words: A Compendium of Conjurations, British Folk Magic, and Other Popish Charms and has been practicing, alongside researching Folk Magic in its various forms for over 20 years. Originally born in native 'witch country' Essex, he enjoys creating videos for his YouTube channel George Hares which focuses on the magical arts particularly within the traditions of British folk magic and the Old Craft current of Witchcraft. Outside of the occult arts, he enjoys going to the gym, studying language, and gardening.

Find him on YouTube: George Hares
Instagram: thenorthenglishwitch

Made in the USA
Columbia, SC
15 December 2022